Rivers in the Desert

Is God Doing a New Thing?

David Rosebaugh

Contributions by David Smith

Rivers in the Desert: Is God Doing a New Thing?
© 2017 by David Rosebaugh and David Smith
www.RiversInTheDesert.net

All Rights Reserved. Other than occasional page copying for personal use, no part of this document may be reproduced without written permission from the author.

ISBN-13: 978-1981500628
ISBN-10: 1981500626
Printed in the United States of America

Scripture quotations marked AMP are taken from the Amplified® Bible (AMPC), Copyright © 1954, 1958, 1962, 1964, 1965, 1987 by the Lockman Foundation. Used by permission. www.Lockman.org

Scriptures marked ESV are taken from The ESV® Bible (The Holy Bible, English Standard Version®), copyright © 2001 by Crossway, a publishing ministry of Good News Publishers.
Used by permission. All rights reserved.

Scripture quotations marked NIV are taken from the Holy Bible, New International Version®, NIV®. Copyright © 1973, 1978, 1984, 2011 by Biblica, Inc.™ Used by permission of Zondervan. All rights reserved worldwide.

Scripture quotations marked NKJV taken from the New King James Version®. Copyright © 1982 by Thomas Nelson. Used by permission. All rights reserved.

Scripture quotations marked NLT are taken from the Holy Bible, New Living Translation, copyright © 1996, 2004, 2015 by Tyndale House Foundation. Used by permission of Tyndale House Publishers, Inc., Carol Stream, Illinois 60188. All rights reserved.

Scripture quotations marked MSG are taken from The Message, copyright © 1993, 1994, 1995, 1996, 2000, 2001, 2002 by Eugene H. Peterson. Used by permission of NavPress. All rights reserved.

Scripture quotations marked TPT are taken from *Letters from Heaven by the Apostle Paul*, The Passion Translation®, copyright 2014. Used by permission of BroadStreet Publishing Group, LLC, Racine, Wisconsin, USA. All rights reserved.

Contents

Introduction 1
Part One Rivers in the Church 3
    What Is Reformation? 4
    Reformation of Belief 11
    Double Violation by David Smith 22
    Reformation of Practice 26
    Gathering 30
    Equipping 40
    Going 67
    21st Century Church 80
Part Two Rivers in My Life 93
    Early Days 94
    Experiencing God 105
    Growth 118
    Finish Well 123
    Revival in Minnesota by David Smith 128
Part Three Rivers in Your Life 135
    What Is Your Dream? 136
    What Is Your Ministry? 141
    Pursuing Your Destiny 145

Dedication

I once gave my testimony by giving credit to the four people who had most impacted my faith.

The earliest was my Dad, Howard Rosebaugh, a charismatic Presbyterian pastor who moved in gifts of healing.

In my twenties, God brought my dear wife, Deb. She has walked with me through "thick and thin" for almost 50 years. Deb embodies never-ending encouragement and love. Her smile lights up the room.

Deb is the primary author of the chapter, "Identity of the Believer."

In my thirties, God took me to a man named Lyle, who diligently discipled me through my "early days" of pursuing the Lord.

In my forties, God introduced me to a prophetic friend, David Smith. His word to us in the early 1990s and his continuing support were a major catalyst for this book.

David is the author of chapters titled "Double Violation," "Rehearse, Rehearse, Rehearse," "The Discerning Heart," and "Revival in Minnesota."

I dedicate this book to these four. Jesus has blessed me powerfully through each of them.

Thanks

I am thankful to literally dozens of friends and church leaders who have spoken into my life over the years. Our many conversations at all hours of the day and night helped form my thoughts. Of course, aside from chapters by my co-authors, I alone am responsible for the words on these pages.

Four men deserve special thanks for motivating me to put my thoughts in a book.

In 2009, I encountered Harold Eberle on a business trip to Washington state. Harold invited us to his home, displaying wonderful hospitality to a total stranger. Harold suggested a visit to his friend, John Garfield, who co-authored with Harold a book on marketplace ministry.

In 2010, we met Deb's cousin, Steve Schroeder, who heads the Christian Ministers Association of Canada. Our heart alignment launched a close friendship. We regularly sit and talk about Jesus for hours at a time.

In 2017, John Garfield spoke at Harold's annual conference in Yakima. He told the audience, "you can write a book." God whispered to my heart, "that means you."

The final nudge to write came from reading a book by Garris Elkins, a lifelong pastor and leader in the Foursquare church. On a whim, I contacted him to meet for coffee. He offered excellent practical advice.

Thank you, Harold, Steve, John, and Garris. I thank each of you for your heart, your example, and your words of encouragement.

Introduction

> *Behold, I will do a new thing,*
> *Now it shall spring forth;*
> *Shall you not know it?*
> *I will even make a road in the wilderness*
> *And rivers in the desert.*
> *I give waters in the wilderness*
> *And rivers in the desert,*
> *To give drink to My people, My chosen.*
> *Isaiah 43:19-20 (NKJV)*

Isaiah penned these words at a time when the nation of Israel was in exile, captive to Babylon. God intended these words to bring hope to the people of Israel. God did indeed do a new thing for them – releasing them from captivity, and returning them to their Promised Land.

History shows more than one case of God doing a new thing – giving rivers in the desert for his people to find refreshment. He did this with Jesus, who brought "rivers of living water" to a thirsty people. He did it again in the time of Martin Luther and others. These men brought to a dry religious world a "new thing" in the form of the Protestant Reformation.

Might God be doing a "new thing" in our day, a new initiative intended to give refreshing waters to God's people?

I will pursue this question from three perspectives.

Part One, "Rivers in the Church," explores what God is doing in the church-at-large. I outline changes in

Introduction

both what is taught and how we gather. Some consider these changes a new reformation.

Part Two, "Rivers in My Life," takes a more personal approach. I use stories to illustrate "rivers" in my life. This includes themes of personal revival, intimacy with God, and pursuing a call and destiny.

Part Three, "Rivers in Your Life," invites you, the reader, to consider your personal dream and ministry. What God is doing for me he is doing for others. What God is doing in the church-at-large applies to the life of every believer.

Part One
Rivers in the Church

What Is Reformation?

In this section, I examine the difference between revival and true reformation. I will consider whether it makes a difference, and say that God is the one who decides.

More Than Revival?

In the late 1990s, I taught a course on the *History of the Great Revivals*. The church has seen many revivals in two thousand years. By revival, I mean "new life" after a period of decline. The Bible contains many examples of revival. In the Old Testament, leaders in the book of Judges brought revival to a nation in decline. Several kings of the Old Testament brought revival after earlier kings wandered away from God.

In the course I taught, we first studied Pentecost. Then we looked at Luther, Wesley, the First and Second Great Awakenings in America, the Welsh Revival, Azusa Street, and more. Some of these could be called Reformation rather than Revival. Is there a difference? The English prefix "re" means "again." So re-vive means life again, or new life. Likewise, re-form means form again, or new form. Of course, simple English definitions do not capture the full implications of these words.

Revival

Revival starts in the church. Spiritual manifestations are common in revival meetings. At Wesley's meetings,

More Than Revival?

people would "swoon" as the message reached their hearts. Today we call it being "slain in the Spirit." Revival meetings in the 20th century included many spiritual manifestations. Those manifestations, in places such as Toronto and Brownsville, were often controversial.

Revival brings a flurry of activity. It brings an increase in salvations and a fervency of faith that can spill over into the community. In the Welsh revival of the early 1900s, crime ceased in many towns as the churches filled with seekers. But a decade later, life in the towns and villages had returned to what it was before the revival.

Regrettably, the history of revival shows that they are often short-lived, lasting at most several years. Sustained change only comes through reformation, where belief patterns and church structures undergo a major shift. Progress in reformation is often slow because the changes are so far-reaching.

Reformation

Reformation may start in the church, but the impact is broader and lasts longer. Reformation impacts culture in a region or nation. Reformation involves fundamental changes in the beliefs and practices of the church. The original Pentecost in 30 AD launched reformation. In the 1500s, Luther ushered in dramatic and long-lasting changes in belief and practice.

Luther's reformation in Germany went on for decades. Over time, it produced the Lutheran denomina-

What Is Reformation?

tion, which spread throughout Germany and Scandinavia. Calvin's reformation in Switzerland spread to Scotland through John Knox. It produced the Presbyterian and other reformed church denominations. In England, during the 1700s, John Wesley sought changes in the Anglican church before he was expelled. After decades of independent work he formed the Methodist Church. Both Luther and Wesley sought reformation *within* the church before being forced out. Each man had no choice but to pursue reformation outside the existing church structure.

What does the church need today? What is God doing today?

Do We Need Another Reformation?

Many observers say that the church in America is not as vibrant as it could be. Recent studies have indicated that as many as 80% of churches in America have plateaued or are in decline.

In the last century, God sent revival to America several times. In the early 1900s, revival at Azusa Street brought a new Pentecost to the world. The impact on society was so significant and widespread that Azusa could even be called a reformation.

Later, in mid-century, God sent revival through such movements as the Latter Rain, Full Gospel Business Men's Fellowship, and Jesus People. At the end of the century, revival broke out in Toronto, Ontario and Brownsville, Florida.

Revivals like these seem much like the experience of Israel in the time of the Judges. We see an outpouring of God's presence and glory, impacting thousands, followed by a season of relative complacency. Do we need another revival? Or, does the church in America need another reformation?

This subject began to interest me over thirty years ago, as I read tracts authored by a well-known musician, Keith Green. Green published several tracts about Charles Finney, a key figure in the Second Great Awakening in America. In town after town, revival came when Finney preached. Some give this spiritual awakening credit for strengthening the abolitionist movement before the Civil War. Many disagree with Finney's

What Is Reformation?

theology or methods, but he brought revival to a complacent church.

My fascination with revival ran about fifteen years. During this time, we were active in three different churches. We also immersed ourselves in three different home groups. These home groups wrestled with patterns we observed in the contemporary church. In our view, church life fell far short of what happens in revival. We wanted to see people coming to salvation, leading to a deep hunger for God. We wanted to see Christians spending time with other believers outside Sunday morning. We wanted to see Christians yearning to share their faith with others.

During our journey, we discovered authors who offered their critique of the contemporary church. They attributed the "lukewarm" faith of many Christians to several factors. They saw superficial salvation, poor discipleship, and structure based on secular business models.

For our friends and us, a frequent question during this time was how to pursue God. Should we be active in a local church, or should we step outside the "organized" church and see what God would do with us? We tried both approaches, experiencing blessing and frustration in both.

Along the way, we encountered quite a few people "hurt by the church." I explore this theme in the chapter, "Hurt by the Church." From time to time we had our own experiences with the shortcomings of our church leaders. It's tempting at those times to think "we can do it better." But the reality of the human condition is that

Do We Need Another Reformation?

weaknesses in our brothers and sisters will lead to others being hurt. It can happen inside a local church or in a home group that is outside a local church. The issues may be different. But all of us must learn how to process what others say and do in a mature way. As we move toward maturity, we will learn to forgive, learn to distinguish words and actions from motives, and learn that being offended is a choice. We do not have to be offended. It truly is a choice.

When you reach a degree of personal freedom, learning not to be offended by the weaknesses of the church, you face an interesting question. You ask yourself, will I just adjust my expectations and be content with the church as it is? Or, will I do what I can to contribute toward revival? Or, should I find some way to pursue reformation in the church?

The year 2017 is the 500th anniversary of Luther posting his 95 Theses. That event launched the Protestant Reformation. What is God doing in the twenty-first century? Has God been laying the groundwork for a new reformation? What does an individual or a small group of individuals do if they feel led to pursue reformation?

What Is Reformation?
God is the Author of Reformation

We know from scripture that Jesus builds the church (Matthew 16:18). But he uses men and women to do the work. Consider Luther. God was ready to bring about change in the church. For God, the practice of indulgences seemed to be the "last straw." But he used a man, Martin Luther to do the work. Luther formulated 95 Theses and posted them on the church door in Wittenburg. Luther stood before the judge and declared that he could take no other stand. Luther translated the Bible into German, the language of the people so that everyone could read scripture for themselves.

Luther brought a reformation of salvation by grace through faith, rather than salvation through works. In this season, the 500th anniversary of Luther's reformation, there seems to be a new reformation of grace. As in Luther's time, many Christians focus on doing the right things. These vary by church, but for most, the "right things" include going to church, giving an offering, and trying to live the Christian life. As in Luther's time, most of the work of ministry is done by ordained clergy. As in Luther's time, many churches are in maintenance mode, investing most of their resources in holding meetings for members.

If God is ushering in a new reformation, he will bring a set of contrasting beliefs and practices to the church. Looking at the past twenty years, we can see several contrasting ideas gaining influence in the church. In the next chapters, we will explore several "new" ideas that are gaining influence in the church.

Reformation of Belief

In this section, I outline three beliefs that have gained influence in recent decades. They are Father's love, the identity of the believer, and empowering grace.

Three Beliefs

In 1517, God launched a reformation of the church through the efforts of Martin Luther. The Protestant Reformation was a re-formation of both belief and practice. These are inter-related. The practice of indulgences (paying money to the church for the dead) was based on a doctrine of purgatory (a "holding area" for the dead short of heaven).

Nonetheless, it will be helpful to distinguish between belief and practice. For example, today the idea of meeting for church in a home or coffee shop is associated with a belief in the "priesthood of the believer." This was a major doctrine of the Protestant Reformation. A contemporary understanding of this idea is that any individual can bring something to share at a meeting.

> *Speak to one another with psalms, hymns and spiritual songs. Ephesians 5:19a (NIV)*

> *Well, my brothers and sisters, let's summarize. When you meet together, one will sing, another will teach, another will tell some special revelation God has given, one will speak in tongues, and another will interpret what is said. But everything that is*

Reformation of Belief

done must strengthen all of you. 1 Corinthians 14:26 (NLT)

This belief in the "priesthood of the believer" and the practice of home church do not always go together. A home church may be led by a single person who gives little room for others to contribute. And a church assembly of 100 can offer the freedom for anyone in the meeting to bring a "word" to the assembly.

Because belief and practice are not always linked, I will explore themes of belief first, followed by themes of practice.

Any attempt to make a list of themes that God has brought to the church in the last twenty years is inherently subjective. What is "new" to me may be a lifelong practice to you. More importantly, a new belief that I feel was brought to me by God may be "heresy" to you. For many, an idea may be "heresy" because it doesn't line up with the teachings of the church they attend. In this situation, it doesn't help to point out that Luther was considered a heretic by the church of his day. None of us think that we have heretical beliefs, or we wouldn't hang on to the belief.

What follows are short summaries of three beliefs that have been important in our lives. This book is not the place for extended discussion of these beliefs. There are many good books and online resources for each one.

Father's Love

John 3:16 declares Father's love for us: "For God so loved the world." This kind of love is unconditional, unrelated to performance. But it's a challenge for many Christians to believe God loves them this way. It is too easy to interpret the ups and downs of life as a reflection of the well-known phrase, spoken by the young as they hold a daisy: "He loves me, he loves me not." Many people go so far as to say, how can there be a God when so many bad things happen in the world? Even a believing Christian can think this way, when efforts to serve God seem to go wrong, or not produce the expected blessing.

Hopefully, we come to believe that God truly loves us, despite circumstances. Then, despite our ups and downs, we come to the place of wanting intimacy with Father. This idea has gained influence over the past twenty years. Now, many Christians understand the value and pleasure of spending time with Father.

This theme of Father's love began to emerge in the late 20th century, partly through the outpouring at the Toronto Airport Vineyard church. Related themes include intimacy with Father and our identity as sons and daughters.

We recommend these books for more information on Father's love:

The Father Heart of God, by Floyd McClung
Experiencing Father's Embrace, by Jack Frost
Fathered by God, by John Eldredge (for men)

Reformation of Belief

Identity of the Believer

We have a new identity in Jesus. Paul's statement in his letter to the Galatians makes this clear.

> *My old identity has been crucified with Christ and no longer lives; for the nails of his cross crucified me with him. And now the essence of this new life is no longer mine, for Christ lives his life through me — we live in union as one! My new life is empowered by the faith of the Son of God who loves me so much that he gave himself for me, and dispenses his life into mine! Galatians 2:20 (TPT)*

This theme is closely related to the Fatherhood of God. We are sons and daughters of Father, and brothers and sisters of Christ. We are kings and priests. We are saints.

If you grew up in the church, you were taught that you were saved by grace. Salvation was offered as a gift. But then, in many churches, we were told that we didn't measure up. We learned that sanctification came by "keeping the law." The law was a set of standards of behavior.

This may not be your experience. But our experience as parents was being told that our kids didn't measure up, and that it was our fault. We were told that a good parent would control the behavior of their kids, to make sure they conformed to the expected standards. Finger-pointing was prevalent. It didn't matter that no one could keep the law. The Apostle Paul, who had been a

Identity of the Believer

Pharisee, wrote a letter to the Galatians to make that clear. Paul could not keep the law, and turned to Christ to rescue him!

Even when no human accused us, the enemy of our soles was happy to send accusations, the fiery darts of Ephesians 6.

All of us fall short of religious standards. Like most of the church, we believed we were "sinners saved by grace." But that phrase is nowhere in the New Testament. Instead, the Bible uses the term "saints" for believers in several local churches, including those in Corinth, Philippi, and Rome.

Paul told the Romans,

> *Even so consider yourselves also dead to sin and your relation to it broken, but alive to God [living in unbroken fellowship with Him] in Christ Jesus. Romans 6:11 (AMP)*

Paul's letter to the Corinthians addresses many shortcomings and sin patterns in that church. Yet he begins the letter by calling them saints.

> *To the church (assembly) of God which is in Corinth, to those consecrated and purified and made holy in Christ Jesus, [who are] selected and called to be saints (God's people), together with all those who in any place call upon and give honor to the name of our Lord Jesus Christ, both their Lord and ours: 1 Corinthians 1:2 (AMP)*

Reformation of Belief

We Are Saints

What does it mean to be saints? Too many Christians see themselves alternating between committing sin and receiving forgiveness. Indeed, the liturgy used in some major denominations includes weekly confession and forgiveness.

It's time to see ourselves as a "new creation," with a new identity. One key to understanding our identity as a believer is to read the Bible and believe what it says. Here are some phrases you can say out loud, based on what the Bible says.

> *Old things have passed away. All things have become new. 2 Corinthians 5:17 (NKJV)*

> *I'm the righteousness of God in Christ Jesus. (Based on 2 Corinthians 5:21.)*

Focus on the one that is alive! It may seem like a subtle difference, but it's not. We are to live from our new life, not our old. The old self has been crucified with Christ and died, and God is not dealing with it anymore. When we make sin our focus, we are trying to resurrect our old, dead self. Your new man is your true nature!

Let's put our focus on the one that is living. What you focus on, you empower. What you lean into, you move toward. What you behold, you become.

As we increasingly understand our identity, it will revolutionize our perception of ourselves. When we see ourselves as righteous saints rather than miserable sinners, we are better able to act like the saints we are.

Identity of the Believer

When we see ourselves having authority in Jesus and power through the Holy Spirit, we are more likely to see the "greater works" Jesus said we would do.

We recommend this book for more information on identity of the believer:

Who We Are in Christ, by Joe McIntyre

Grace

Some would say that our new identity is only a potential identity, one that we spend the rest of our lives working toward. Yes, there is a process of becoming all that God says we are. But if we're not careful, we fall back into "try harder" Christianity, where our focus is on using willpower. When we do that, we look to ideas of positive and negative reinforcement borrowed from the field of psychology.

For centuries, Christians have approached changed behavior through rules of behavior supported by personal discipline. This approach is based on the power of the soul (mind, will, emotions) to accomplish change. Sometimes it works. But many Christians have struggled against certain behaviors without finding victory. Too often the gospel message offers salvation by faith followed by a life of sanctification by willpower and discipline.

Although the intentions are good for "try harder" Christianity, it leads to a performance mindset. Too often we feel we don't measure up, and much of the preaching and teaching we experience encourages that feeling. In some respects, a focus on performance is based in legalism – keep these rules to please God.

Many Christians have found freedom from what they perceive as legalism through the truth of empowering grace.

The church has understood grace as unmerited favor since the time of Luther.

Empowering Grace

Within the last twenty years, we see more and more teaching on the empowering nature of grace.

One author, James Ryle, defined it this way: "Grace is the empowering Presence of God enabling you to be who He created you to be, and to do what He has called you to do." Another author, Graham Cooke, says this: "Grace is the empowering presence of God that enables you to become the person that He sees when He looks at you."

These definitions point to a new understanding of grace. Empowering grace points to a different life, with change realized by the power of the Holy Spirit inside us. This includes a changed understanding of who we are in Christ.

This view of grace is labeled "hyper-grace" by some in the church. They criticize hyper-grace as excusing sin. We do not hold to this view of grace. Hopefully, this controversy will resolve in time.

Luther's view of grace brought controversy. In the end, a better understanding of grace emerged. God is doing this again.

In my view, true grace is the power to think and do what is right. For many years I have taught grace based on this scripture.

> *For the grace of God that brings salvation has appeared to all men. It teaches us to say "No" to ungodliness and worldly passions, and to live self-controlled, upright and godly lives in this present age,*
> *Titus 2:11-12 (NIV)*

Reformation of Belief

God's standards of righteousness have not changed. But through the truth of empowering grace, the path we walk and the power we use for living in righteousness is changing.

Changes in our thinking and actions are the outworking of God's spirit in our lives. We are changed, not by the power of the soul (mind, will, and emotions), but by the grace of God through the power of Holy Spirit.

We recommend these resources for more information on God's grace:

Destined to Reign, by Joseph Prince
Sanctification by Grace, by Ryan Rufus
www.empoweringgraceministries.org

Reformation of Belief and the Trinity

These three themes, Father's love, the identity of the believer, and grace, point to a deeper understanding of the Father, the Son, and the Holy Spirit. Now, in the 21st century, we may have a deeper understanding than we've had for the past two thousand years. Are these themes so significant that they could be considered the basis of a reformation?

While these themes are founded on Biblical doctrine, they are also experiential. We experience Father through intimacy, through feeling his delight in us. We view ourselves as like Christ, which is the basic definition of "Christian." We see changes in our behavior by allowing the Holy Spirit to nudge us in areas where change is needed, and saying, "yes, I want that." This is a simple approach to faith.

Do these new ideas constitute a new reformation? Only time will tell. But it is worth exploring what church would look like if we pursued these themes and their implications for church practice.

Double Violation
by David Smith

This section uses a modern parable to bring together the themes of Father's love, identity, and grace.

Double Violation – Plugging the Meter

I was in a conversation the other night, and an analogy of the life of religious performance came to mind.

Here is the picture. I said, "Your life is like a person who pulls up to a parking meter. To feel good about yourself you must put in a quarter. The meter only gives you 15 minutes of peace and security, your 15 minutes in the sun, 15 minutes of approval. Fifteen short minutes later, it demands another quarter for you to stay there, in your happy place. Without your performance (another quarter) the flag will come back up declaring in big red letters, "Violation!"

Many religious people live right there, parked and plugging the meter.

They want God's love, but have missed the entire message of the good news! Plugging money into the offering basket, or plugging time volunteering to "park in his presence" on Sunday morning, was not what God had in mind when he started the church.

Double Violation – Plugging the Meter

The good news is not that you can earn God's love. It is that long before you knew about or cared about anybody but yourself, God lavished his love on you and redeemed you for fellowship with him.

In fact, God so loved you, that he… ummm, well… that he gave his only Son as a ransom for you!

And Jesus did not come into the world to condemn you, but that through him you might have the joy of living forever as his close friend.

So why then the title, "Double Violation"?

Because it is one thing to have never heard nor understood the good news that God loves you and has saved you from sin and death because of the righteousness of his son. In other words, to be living a hopeless life outside of God. To live "without God, without hope in the world" is a "Single Violation."

But it so much more profound to have tasted the presence and love of God and then find yourself back at the parking meter, feeding it quarters to keep "earning the right" to "park in the presence."

Don't Go Back

The writer to the Galatians puts it this way, "Who bewitched you, who painted the wrong picture for you? Having begun your new life by the power of the Spirit, are you going to go back from that freedom and evidence of a life hidden in God and return to the beggarly and weak elements of plugging the meter!" I can almost hear Paul shouting: "Where is the *good news* in that?"

You received Jesus for your salvation with gladness, and you felt so free, so clean. But in the end, is he no

Double Violation
by David Smith

more than a silver dollar instead of my measly quarters? Giving me an hour of freedom instead of the fifteen minutes I could procure by myself? I don't think so!

The writer in Hebrews contrasts the gospel with the old way of perpetual sacrifices to temporarily cover our sins. Peter explains that we were not redeemed by gold coins, by silver or any corruptible (temporary) thing, but rather with the precious blood of Jesus the Christ (1 Peter 1:18-19). Christ's sacrifice was not temporary, like the blood of sheep and goats, but was given once for all and for all time.

The parking meter (law) was our tutor to bring us to faith in God, not the other way around.

Picture this. We find an antique store that still has a few of these parking meters in the back room. They purchased them from the city when the city officials pulled them from the streets. They still had a few repaired units in the maintenance department, which they kept ready to replace a broken or missing meter. We are so excited to see a familiar friend. Perhaps a familiar spirit. We buy it! With our own money. We hire someone to cement it into the curb in front of our house! And now we make a pilgrimage twice a week and put another quarter in the meter. And all the time, in our hearts, we accuse God of being a harsh taskmaster, and we wonder about our hard life and ask, where is the joy of my salvation?

The Double Violation is returning to the weak and beggarly elements (Galatians 4:9), returning to performance and repeated self-sacrifice in order to inherit Kingdom privileges.

Double Violation – Plugging the Meter

Instead, God urges us, "Believe in the Lord Jesus Christ, and you shall be saved" (Act 16:31).

God declares a salvation by grace through faith. Jesus not only plugged the meter for us, he permanently, but also removed them from every street in the city and cast them into the sea of forgetfulness! He did that so that we cannot go back to the former way.

Jesus and only Jesus is our Jubilee – our Freedom.

Reformation of Practice

In this section, I introduce three practices that have gained influence in recent decades. I will describe each in more detail in later sections.

Three Practices

In the previous section, I outlined three themes of belief God has brought to the church in recent decades. Do preaching and teaching on these themes produce a change in practice? Has God brought changes to how we "do church" at the same time as he has brought changes in our beliefs? I believe the answer to these questions is yes.

One way to answer such questions is to ask people how they are doing church. We can ask our friends, who are likely to be doing what we are doing. But asking a larger number of Christians should yield helpful information. For many decades, a research pollster named George Barna took the pulse of American Christians on a wide variety of topics. In 2005, he published a book titled *Revolution*. This book explored alternative ways Christians had decided to "do church" and "be church."

Barna reviewed some of the frustrations Christians experience in their local churches. He identified several alternatives that believers are exploring. These include organic church, simple church, house church, emerging church, marketplace gatherings, and cyber church. Each

Three Practices

of these has their benefits and drawbacks, but the point is that people are exploring options.

Many of these new alternatives focus on one facet of church life. Some emphasize fellowship, gathering in homes and spending extended time in relationship. Some emphasize prayer, even to the point of houses of prayer, such as the International House of Prayer (IHOP). Some emphasize going and doing, such as ministry in the streets. Some emphasize extended worship, such as Hillsong Church in Australia. Any time there is an emphasis on one facet of church there can be a shift away from patterns of the past. For example, in many of these new alternative patterns, the themes of fathering and the identity of the believer are strong.

In this way, new themes of belief brought by God to the church may encourage new patterns of gathering, with old patterns abandoned over time. We can't be sure that new theology drives new meeting patterns. But it seems clear that those who pursue new beliefs are also likely to pursue new meeting patterns.

Might God also be bringing changes to how we "do church" beyond changes that result from new beliefs? I believe the answer is yes, since a change in activities in meetings does not have to be rooted in changes in beliefs.

Summarized below are three practices that my friends and I have discovered in the past thirty years: gathering, equipping, and going. Jesus spent much of his time in a small fellowship of the twelve. He equipped them to go places, and then sent them. These practices are core elements of the church in Acts.

Reformation of Practice

Gathering

The early church had several patterns for gathering as church, as described in Acts 2.

> *They committed themselves to the teaching of the apostles, the life together, the common meal, and the prayers.* Acts 2:42 (MSG)

The church has always done a good job with teaching. Many local churches offer small group fellowships on the church calendar. Many find "the life together" at such meetings. But there is more to experiencing true friendship and fellowship than simply gathering in a small group. I wonder if the decline of the weekly meeting for prayer in most churches reflects lives lived at a distance rather than "life together." In my experience, the most powerful prayer results when we are deeply engaged in the lives of fellow believers.

I explore this theme in several chapters in the next section, "Gathering," beginning with "Fellowships of the Heart."

Equipping

In the Great Commission, Jesus told the disciples to go places ("all nations") and make disciples (Matthew 28:19-20). Before saints go places and make disciples, they need training and equipping. This mirrors what Jesus did with his twelve disciples. Jesus explained and illustrated what he wanted them to do, and then sent them out to do it. Leaders in the contemporary church have the same assignment. Leaders can help believers to learn and grow into this role. I explore this theme in several chapters in the section, "Equipping," beginning with "Builders."

Going

At the end of his time on earth, Jesus told the disciples to go places and make disciples. He intends us to do the same. Yet statistics show that many Christians seldom or never share their faith. The message we hear in most churches is that we should invite others to church. In other words, the message is "come in" rather than "go out." This is not true of all churches, and it is changing. I explore this theme in several chapters in the section "Going," beginning with "The Great Commission."

Gathering

This section examines the practice of gathering together. I discuss the challenges when people struggle to get along, especially when passions are involved.

Fellowships of the Heart

For most Christians "church" is a Sunday morning meeting in a building designed for that purpose. The building is such a focal point that when we use the word "church," we typically mean the building where we meet.

In the New Testament, the word for Christians gathering together is *ekklesia*. In all but one case, this is translated into the English word "church." Unfortunately, the word "church" comes from the Latin word chirche, which referred to a religious building.

An *ekklesia* was not a religious building. The one time the word is not translated "church" reflects the meaning of the word. In Acts 19:32, a group of Ephesians gathered in the amphitheater to riot. Their purpose was not Christian assembly. But they were a gathering of people for a purpose, which is the meaning of *ekklesia*.

When the church of Christ formed early in the book of Acts, the focal point was teaching, fellowship, gathering together around a meal, and prayer.

Fellowships of the Heart

They committed themselves to the teaching of the apostles, the life together, the common meal, and the prayers. Acts 2:42 (MSG)

All the believers devoted themselves to the apostles' teaching, and to fellowship, and to sharing in meals (including the Lord's Supper), and to prayer. Acts 2:42 (NLT)

As my wife and I pursued God beyond the hour-on-Sunday-morning pattern, we discovered the blessing of small group fellowship. At first, we joined small groups sponsored by the local church we attended. During most of the 1980s, we joined the young couples in our church, gathering monthly as a "Collection of Friends." Our activities were a mix of food, fellowship, and fun.

Later, we found couples who shared a common perspective with us, and we gathered in each other's homes.

For us, this idea was best expressed in a book we read in 2006. In *Waking the Dead*, John Eldredge wrote a chapter, "Fellowships of the Heart," in which he talks about church as community. I have borrowed the term from him. He wrote that such fellowships are outposts of the Kingdom.

You can find many books about small groups. When sponsored by a local church, they are often called home groups or life groups. When independently formed, they are often called house churches. There are often distinctions between these approaches, in leadership and structure, but that is not the focus here.

Gathering

Over the past thirty years, we have been part of about ten small group fellowships. Most of these formed spontaneously, by God prompting people to invite others. It has been our privilege to sit with gifted friends around a circle. We have experienced in them gifts of worship, prophecy, teaching, healing, and shepherding. Of course, we brought our gift to the circle. As a result, we all learned from one another.

At its best, a small group can offer much of what is often lacking in the Sunday morning meeting. In one group, we would linger in prayer for as long as three hours. This same group offered a pattern of pastoring one another. As each one shared a need, others would bring words of comfort, counsel, and even correction in an atmosphere of love and friendship.

A small group can also teach the more difficult lessons of Christianity, such as how to handle conflict. Many small groups "blow up" while learning these lessons. That painful experience also offers a lesson. We learn to ask, is the relationship more important than being right on the issue? I explore this topic in the next chapter, "Do I Need to Be Right?" We know from the history of the church, especially the Protestant church, that Christians have often chosen "being right" over relationship. That seems to be changing within the past few years. There are now excellent teachings on how to deal with conflict, including *Foundations of Honor*, by Danny Silk.

Do I Need to Be Right?

I have a confession to make. I like to be right, or at least think that I am right. Often when I find myself in a disagreement with a fellow believer, an urge bubbles up inside me to point out where I am right, and my brother or sister is wrong. As you might guess, this seldom goes well.

I am still learning why this happens. Like most readers of this book, I'm a product of Western culture. In other cultures, people find it easier to have a conversation that includes disagreements without letting it affect their relationship. As evidence of how we in Western culture handle disagreements, consider that there are thousands of Protestant denominations. Martin Luther launched one of them. The rest have come as some Protestants disagreed with other Protestants, and dealt with it by going their separate ways.

For me, there are other contributing factors. I grew up with an evangelical approach to faith. I was taught to pursue righteousness. This meant I should avoid "wrong" and pursue "right" thoughts, words, and actions. While this perspective is biblical, the problem comes when you apply to others what God has shown you as "right." We should let the Holy Spirit convict others of what is right or wrong in their life.

Although my evangelical perspective was a factor, what made it worse was a perfectionist tendency in my personality. I have always been one to want my "ducks in a row." I spent 30 years writing computer software, where being a perfectionist is helpful. It is not helpful in relationships.

These are all excuses for my need to be right, and there is no excuse. That's why Holy Spirit has been

Gathering

working on this tendency in me for a long time. There is some progress. God gives me an incentive to change by showing me the damage I cause to relationships. This is how he has changed me in many ways over the years – he shows me a better way to be and asks if I want that. Usually, I do, and then he changes me, from the inside out. This is what I called "empowering grace" in an earlier chapter. This process impacts many areas of behavior. This is the consistent pattern I have seen as Father works in me to produce fruit. I further explore this theme in the chapter, "The Gardener."

I look for the day when I can disagree without being disagreeable. Another way to say it is that I want to contrast right and wrong only when God says I should. That was the standard for Martin Luther in the original Reformation. May it be our standard today.

Hurt by the Church

All of us know folks who have been "hurt by the church," and from time to time we may have personally experienced hurt feelings. When disagreements come along, as we discussed in the last chapter, one or both parties often feel hurt. Why does this happen, and what can we do about it? I'll offer a few observations, although others have more wisdom about this than me.

People get hurt when someone else does something they regard as offensive. What hurts us reflects our relative maturity in God. Less mature Christians may get "hurt" when a leader offers correction. This is similar to the way a young child may be reluctant to receive correction from a parent. But leaders also get hurt, as when someone betrays them.

I believe God chooses to allow hurtful situations to arise. Some time ago Gene Edwards wrote a book titled *Crucified by Christians*. Edwards says we are most easily hurt by those we trust, those in our (church) family. We expected them to act kindly towards us (based on our understanding of kindness), and, in our view, they did not. We can hope a day will come when people don't get hurt, but that is not realistic. God is trying to teach us something when hurtful situations come along. Until we are completely dead to offenses, hurts will come.

There is excellent teaching available from many teachers about how to deal with hurts or offenses. John Bevere's "Bait of Satan" teaching is a good place to start.

We must be careful not to criticize people who feel hurt about something that happened to them. That's like

Gathering

telling someone who doesn't get healed after prayer that they must not have enough faith. A person does not get over hurt by being told they shouldn't be feeling hurt.

Often the things that hurt us are pointing us to a place in our heart that needs a deeper ministry of healing. Many of us, for example, have not yet come to the place of trusting that God is good all the time. Why? Often this is because "bad" things happen that we can't explain. When God allows hurts to come into our lives, his real purpose is to heal us. That's why it's so important to learn how to handle hurtful situations.

Homothumadon

During the times I pursue in-depth Bible study, I usually pull up my Bible software on my computer. Most of what I do is now available online at no cost. I still like my older software, partly because I'm familiar with it and it does what I need to do quickly. I especially like the Parallel Bible view, where I can display eight translations side-by-side, and easily make comparisons. With eight translations, I can see the word-by-word perspective contrasted with the phrase-by-phrase wording. It helps me understand better what is meant by a verse or phrase. One of the eight "translations" I read is *The Message*, by Eugene Peterson. Most would call it a paraphrase. The Message often offers insights that are not readily seen elsewhere.

At some point, I encountered Peterson's book, *The Jesus Way*. In this book, he explores the meaning and significance of *homothumadon*, a Greek word that appears several times in early chapters of Acts. This word is typically translated "of one accord" or "together." Peterson tells us *homothumadon* has fire in it, that it expresses passionate, energetic unity. Here are a few of the verses where the word appears.

> *These all continued with one accord in prayer and supplication, with the women and Mary the mother of Jesus, and with His brothers. Acts 1:14 (NKJV)*
> *When the Day of Pentecost had fully come, they were all with one accord in one place. Acts 2:1 (NKJV)*

Gathering

> *So continuing daily with one accord in the temple, and breaking bread from house to house, they ate their food with gladness and simplicity of heart, Acts 2:46 (NKJV)*

> *So when they heard that, they raised their voice to God with one accord and said: "Lord, You are God, who made heaven and earth and the sea, and all that is in them, Acts 4:24 (NKJV)*

> *And through the hands of the apostles many signs and wonders were done among the people. And they were all with one accord in Solomon's Porch. Acts 5:12 (NKJV)*

The evidence of these verses is that the early church lived in passionate, energetic unity. Surely this passionate unity was a major reason for the rapid growth of the church. Most of us respond more readily to when our leaders are passionate, and when everyone chooses to follow the leaders.

In my experience, passionate, energetic unity is not easy to find. In the Western church, unity is often accomplished by watering down any common agreement, leading to little passion from anyone. On the other hand, as those who hold differing views become more passionate about those views, the less unity we have. With the arrival of the Internet era, it is more and more common to see Christians bashing other Christians in online forums, blogs, and social media. I find this sad.

To be genuine, this passionate, energetic unity must be a work of God. I believe God is bringing insights to the church regarding how to disagree without being disrespectful. But a true state of unity in a passionate church is something to pursue in prayer, with a heart of humility and love towards others.

Equipping

This section examines the challenge of equipping every believer to do ministry. I consider patterns established in the early church, along with contemporary wisdom about teaching and learning.

Builders

As a 7-year old boy, the highlight of my summer days was playing in our sandbox. Naturally, I enjoyed building a treehouse with my dad and hiking in the neighborhood. But my dad built a sandbox with railroad ties at the sides. The sandbox was big – about six by eight feet. The sand was at least a foot deep. I spent hours and hours in the sand, building entire cities, multi-level highways, and more. Is it any wonder in college I chose to get a degree in city planning?

As an adult, we spent some time with a mentor, Arthur Burk, who was knowledgeable about the Romans 12 gifts. These are sometimes called design gifts. They include prophet, servant, teacher, exhorter, giver, ruler, and mercy. They are also called "redemptive" gifts, which are gifts from Father to every person, believer or not. We spent some time with Arthur weighing two gifts as possibilities for my primary gift. In the end, my sandbox experience carried the day, pointing us to the sixth of the seven gifts, the one that loves to build "systems." That gift is leader or ruler, depending on the translation, but it would also be fitting to say builder.

Builders

A builder can find work in many occupations. For many, the word builder hints at a carpenter or one who builds houses. Depending on your interests and skills, you can also build a garden, a go-kart, or an organization. In my case, I spent over 30 years building a software product and a business to sell, train, and support our software.

But what does a builder do in the church? After all, Jesus told the disciples that he would build the church (Matthew 16:18). Is there a place for us in building the church? Paul's letter to the Corinthians makes it clear that the answer is yes.

> *According to the grace of God given to me, like a skilled master builder I laid a foundation, and someone else is building upon it. Let each one take care how he builds upon it. 1 Corinthians 3:10 (ESV)*

In the verses just before and after this, Paul writes about builders in a broader context. He uses metaphors and word pictures. Before the quoted verse, he writes about gardens – planting, watering, and growth.

> *I planted, Apollos watered, but God gave the growth. So neither he who plants nor he who waters is anything, but only God who gives the growth. He who plants and he who waters are one, and each will receive his wages according to his labor. For we are God's fellow workers. You are God's field, God's building. 1 Corinthians 3:6-9 (ESV)*

Equipping

Then, afterward, Paul writes about building with gold, silver, jewels, wood, hay, or straw.

> *Now if anyone builds on the foundation with gold, silver, precious stones, wood, hay, straw – each one's work will become manifest, for the Day will disclose it, because it will be revealed by fire, and the fire will test what sort of work each one has done. If the work that anyone has built on the foundation survives, he will receive a reward. If anyone's work is burned up, he will suffer loss, though he himself will be saved, but only as through fire. 1 Corinthians 3:12-15 (ESV)*

These word pictures point to teachings and actions which are beautiful, precious, and long-lasting. They are contrasted to those which will not last when tested by fire.

What Kind of Builder Am I?

In October 1992, Dennis Cramer, a prophet from Pennsylvania, came to our city in Minnesota. A group of a hundred believers from several local churches gathered in a public conference room to hear his message. At the end of his message, he moved into prophetic ministry, calling various individuals and couples to the front. He then circulated in the room to speak to others. My wife and I received a prophetic word from him. He said God had made me a builder, and that I would be part of a team to be a blessing to tens and twenties and thirties.

Builders

At the time I had little understanding of what that might mean. Over the twenty-five years since then, I've studied and explored what it means to be a builder in the church. I've also learned much about "team." The purpose of this book is to contribute in building the church. I join with my brothers and sisters in that purpose, that we may see "rivers in the desert."

What Kind of Builder Are You?

I offer my background as an illustration. As you read the next chapters, ask yourself what kind of builder you are. There are many possibilities, and God will tell you as you seek him.

Equipping

Saints Building

As cited in the last chapter, Paul says that "anyone" can build on the foundation.

> *I laid a foundation, and someone else is building upon it. Now if anyone builds on the foundation...*
> *1 Corinthians 3:10, 12 (ESV)*

Paul describes this pattern more fully later in his letter.

> *What then, brothers? When you come together, each one has a hymn, a lesson, a revelation, a tongue, or an interpretation. Let all things be done for building up. 1 Corinthians 14:26 (ESV)*

All believers are told to bring their gift to the gathering, to build up other believers. Apparently, a meeting of the church in Corinth would be led in turn by several people. Each of them had been equipped by Paul or other church leaders to speak at the meeting. I explored this idea in the chapter, "Fellowships of the Heart."

In most church gatherings, we see a small number of people doing the ministry, leading worship and preaching. What would church gatherings be like if the pastor focused less on *doing* the ministry and more on *equipping* the people for ministry?

What would we equip people to do? One important ministry everyone can do is to share their faith, which I will explore in the chapter, "Sharing Our Faith." Few

Saints Building

Christians share their faith. In some cases, they don't feel they have anything to say. They may be afraid of rejection. They may not know how to steer a conversation toward matters of faith. These barriers can be overcome. Christians can be offered an opportunity to talk about their faith in a small circle of friends. They will then be better prepared to talk about their faith outside the church setting.

How would we do the equipping? We know from the field of education that a lecture leads to limited recall of information. Audio-visual materials help, as does demonstration. Even more effective are discussion groups and practice by doing. I explore the topics of teaching and learning in the chapters, "Learning by Doing" and "The Acts 2 Lifestyle." Two chapters written by David Smith, "Rehearse, Rehearse, Rehearse" and "The Discerning Heart," give examples of role-playing as a learning tool.

The early church was clearly effective at the task of equipping the saints. Acts 8:4 tells us that they went everywhere preaching the good news.

> *Forced to leave home base, the Christians all became missionaries. Wherever they were scattered, they preached the Message about Jesus. Acts 8:4 (MSG)*

The early believers turned the world upside down, according to Acts 17:6. Can we do what they did?

What would the builders of the contemporary church do to equip the saints? Here are some thoughts

Equipping

on what we could do to support the equipping assignment.

- Work with small groups (Jesus trained twelve).
- Ensure active participation of each member of the group.
- Provide feedback and encouragement.
- Teach each person who they are in Christ.
- Teach each person how to share their experiences with the unchurched.
- Encourage each person to bring back stories of their encounters with others.
- Assist each person to identify their spiritual gifting.
- Give opportunity for each person to practice their gifting.

Many churches have small groups, and they may do activities such as these. Some small groups are oriented to teaching, while others focus on fellowship. One way to pursue the ideas listed above would be with a workbook. This is the approach used in the Alpha Course and many other programs designed to teach and train disciples.

Five Equipping Gifts

In his letter to the Ephesians, Paul mentions five kinds of builders. Their purpose is to equip the saints to build.

> *And he gave the apostles, the prophets, the evangelists, the shepherds and teachers, to equip the saints for the work of ministry, for building up the body of Christ, Ephesians 4:11-12 (ESV)*

> *And he has appointed some with grace to be apostles, and some with grace to be prophets, and some with grace to be evangelists, and some with grace to be pastors, and some with grace to be teachers. And their calling is to nurture and prepare all the holy believers to do their own works of ministry, and as they do this they will enlarge and build up the body of Christ. Ephesians 4:11-12 (TPT)*

Paul was both an apostle and a teacher (2 Timothy 1:11). His role as an apostle is that of a "skilled master builder," as he writes in 1 Corinthians 3:10. The skilled master builder was an *architecton*. In Paul's day, this was one who drew up the blueprint, but also served as the general contractor in supervising the construction.

Our focus here is not only on the apostolic role. All five of these kinds of builders are given to the church to equip the saints for the work of ministry. As the saints, God's people, do the work of ministry, they will build up the body of Christ, the church.

Equipping

Some churches believe the gifts of apostle and prophet were only part of the early church, and are no longer applicable. But the purpose of these five gifts is to bring the church to unity and maturity, and everyone would agree that we're not there yet.

Let us consider, then, that all five gifts are still alive in the contemporary church. Many books delve into these gifts, sometimes called the fivefold gifts. This book will not attempt a detailed exploration of them. Even so, here is a summary of the essence of each gift. In each case, I offer short definitions. They come from *Strong's Concordance*, by James Strong, and *Vine's Expository Dictionary*, by W.E. Vine.

Phrases credited to Harold Eberle come from his book, *Complete Wineskin*, and from his spoken messages.

Apostle

Strong's Concordance: ambassador

Vine's Dictionary: one sent forth

Harold Eberle's explanation: an apostle focuses on the work, to change thought patterns in a region

Bible Examples: Jesus called 12 apostles. Other NT apostles include James (Gal 1:19), Paul (numerous references), Barnabas (Acts 14:14), Apollos (1 Corinthians 4:6-9), Timothy and Silas (1 Thessalonians 1:1 with 2:7), Epaphroditus (Philippians 2:25), and others.

Comment: In Roman times, an apostle (Greek *apostolos*) was the admiral of a ship sent to take the Roman culture to a new territory. The ship would include educators, craftsman, and laborers who lived Roman culture. NT apostles were sent forth to take Kingdom culture to the new territories.

Prophet

Strong's Concordance: inspired speaker

Vine's Dictionary: one who speaks a divine message

Harold Eberle's explanation: a prophet focuses on the word, sometimes assisting an apostle by confirmation.

Bible Examples: NT prophets include Agabus (Acts 11:27-8), some at Antioch (Acts 13:1), Judas and Silas (Acts 15:32), and others.

Comment: The fivefold gift of prophet is different from the design gift of prophet (Romans 12:6) and the Holy Spirit manifestation of prophecy which is available to any believer (1 Corinthians 12:10).

Evangelist

Strong's Concordance: preacher of the gospel

Vine's Dictionary: messenger of good news

Harold Eberle's explanation: an evangelist focuses on getting people saved.

Bible Examples: NT evangelists include Philip (Acts 21:8), and others.

Comment: The fivefold gift of evangelist can be distinguished from the responsibility of every believer to share the gospel (Acts 8:4).

Pastor (literally Shepherd)

Strong's Concordance: shepherd

Vine's Dictionary: one who tends flocks

Equipping

Harold Eberle's explanation: a pastor focuses on feeding and protecting the sheep.

Bible Examples: Other than Jesus in 1 Peter 2:25, no New Testament pastors are named. Even so, there were many.

Comment: In Acts 20:28 and 1 Peter 5:1-2, this gift is associated with that of overseer or elder.

Teacher

Strong's Concordance: instructor

Vine's Dictionary: teacher

Harold Eberle's explanation: a teacher focuses on truth.

Bible Examples: NT teachers include Paul (1 Timothy 2:7 and 2 Timothy 1:11), and others (Acts 13:1). There were many others.

Comment: The fivefold gift of teacher should be distinguished from the design gift of teacher (Romans 12:7). One qualification of an elder is to be "able to teach." (1 Timothy 3:2).

Office or Function?

We tend to think of people with one of the five equipping gifts as holding a position or office. This view is understandable, given that most churches are led by a person with the title, Pastor. But this term describes the position. The person in the position may be gifted and function as a prophet or evangelist or teacher rather than a shepherd.

Sometimes a leader of a local church is an administrator, without the gift and grace from God to pastor (shepherd) the people. Such a church may even be quite large. The administrative gift can be effective at keeping the machinery of a church running smoothly.

When we associate the gift with a position, especially a paid position, most of us will assume that a pastor does the "work of a pastor." And what is that work? In most churches, it includes preaching, counseling, visiting the sick, conducting weddings and funerals, and general administration. All of this is good work which needs to be done, but these activities are not the assignment given in Ephesians 4.

Instead, the assignment given to pastors, whatever their fivefold gift, is to equip the saints for the work of the ministry.

> ...*their calling is to nurture and prepare all the holy believers to do their own works of ministry, and as they do this they will enlarge and build up the body of Christ. Ephesians 4:12, (TPT)*

Equipping

To paraphrase, the role of those with a fivefold gift is to equip each of us individually. Yes, an evangelist will evangelize, but the primary assignment is to equip each believer to evangelize. In Acts 8:4, the believers had been equipped to preach the gospel. As a result, the church multiplied.

What might those with other fivefold gifts do?

Prophets will equip believers to hear the Lord, and speak the word of the Lord when appropriate.

Pastors (shepherds) will equip believers to nurture and care for each other.

Teachers will equip believers to study the Word, and grow in their faith.

Apostles will equip believers to take the gospel outside the four walls of the church.

One writer contrasted this apostolic role with the assignment of a pastor. The assignment of a pastor is to equip people to serve in the church. The assignment of an apostle is to equip people to change the world.

Apostolic Teaching

Both preaching and teaching were vital to the early church. Peter preached a message on Pentecost that launched the church (Acts 2:20). The early church devoted themselves to the apostles' teaching (Acts 2:42). This went on for a long time.

> *Day after day, in the temple courts and from house to house, they never stopped teaching and proclaiming the good news that Jesus is the Christ. Acts 5:42 (NIV)*

Today the focus for preaching and teaching is the Sunday morning sermon. How does a 30-minute sermon compare to the early church model?

Studies show that people retain little of what they hear in a spoken message. Later that day, they might remember half of what they heard. A week later, they might remember 10%. These numbers are disputed by some in the education field, but they make sense. Try it yourself. What do you remember today from the sermon you heard last Sunday?

Of course, these studies are looking at how much information people remember. A typical Sunday morning message does include information. But preaching aims higher, to motivate, to inspire, and ultimately to allow the Holy Spirit to change hearts and minds. Those outcomes are very difficult to quantify in a research study. If a person responds to preaching by going to the altar

Equipping

and encountering Jesus as their Savior, the impact is 100%, for eternity.

Let's look again at the percentages. Keep in mind that these are averages. The style of a message affects both what is retained in the head and what is imparted to the heart. For example, the use of stories is helpful. Sometimes the only part of a sermon we remember is the story. The use of visuals helps. Repetition helps. All good preachers know this.

Holy Spirit as Teacher

Ultimately, the Holy Spirit is our teacher, as we know from John's first letter.

> *But you have received the Holy Spirit, and he lives within you, so you don't need anyone to teach you what is true. For the Spirit teaches you everything you need to know, and what he teaches is true – it is not a lie. So just as he has taught you, remain in fellowship with Christ. 1 John 2:27 (NLT)*

In my life, I have experienced Holy Spirit teaching me many principles by asking me to put into practice what I read in my Bible or in a devotional. The practical exercise of a truth has confirmed and "engrafted" the truth in my life. I further explore this idea in the next chapter, "Learning by Doing."

Learning by Doing

All of us want to finish well our walk of faith, to hear "well done, good and faithful servant" from our Lord. Those who study what it takes to finish well point to several factors, among them a commitment to lifelong learning.

Learning is the purpose of teaching. You may be part of a church that offers only lecture-style teaching. Or you may be fortunate to attend a church that offers teaching in a small group discussion format. Whatever format is available to you, the responsibility for learning lies with you, as you are led and taught by Holy Spirit.

When Luke begins his account of Acts, he summarizes the gospel as "everything that Jesus began to do and teach." Jesus spent much of his time teaching his disciples. Then Jesus asked his disciples to do what he had taught them. In Luke 9:2, he sends the twelve out to preach the Kingdom and to heal the sick. In Luke 10:9, he sends the seventy and repeats the assignment. In Matthew 28:19, at the time of his Ascension, he repeats the assignment. He tells the disciples to teach others what Jesus had taught them.

We know they did this. The believers in the early church devoted themselves to the apostles' teaching. This likely happened at the temple, where the stories and teaching offered by the apostles could be heard by hundreds at the same time.

The Great Commission at the end of Matthew was not only for the twelve. It was also for you and me. You

Equipping

and I are commissioned to make disciples and teach them what Jesus taught us.

Before we can teach, we must learn. I've always enjoyed wandering through bookstores. At one time we lived near the campus of a Lutheran college which included a seminary. While browsing through their bookstore, I saw a book of John Wesley's book, *52 Standard Sermons*. Wesley published these sermons so that the Methodist preachers of England and America could preach what he preached. These were the messages that launched the evangelical awakening in England. In these 52 sermons, Wesley covered basic topics of salvation, sanctification, and practical Christian living. He included thirteen messages going into depth on the Sermon on the Mount.

These are topics likely to be taught in most evangelical churches over the course of a year of Sundays. If a disciple of Christ decided to pursue learning in the form of an online Bible school, there are many options available. Most of them assume the student is aiming at credentials for ministry.

What would be included in a series of lessons equipping every Christian, not only leaders, to do the work of the ministry?

This is a different purpose from teaching to impart information. American classrooms are designed to impart knowledge, with a teacher standing at a podium and students lined up in rows of chairs. This teaching format includes quizzes and tests to verify that the student retained the information. By itself, this does not equip the student for doing, for action.

Learning by Doing

One writer illustrated this point with a modern example. Suppose you were studying to be an auto mechanic. If you are only offered lectures in a classroom and never get your hands on a car, it will not go well.

Jesus taught in a way that equipped his students, the disciples, for action. He told stories to illustrate the message, and he demonstrated what he was teaching. Then he asked the disciples to assist him, and finally, he sent them out on their own. And then he "abandoned" them just before the launch of the church at Pentecost.

The coming of Holy Spirit at Pentecost was a critical factor in the launch of the church. But the apostles had learned what Jesus taught. They had learned how to do what Jesus did, and this success resulted from the method of his teaching, "learning by doing." We would do well to teach as Jesus taught.

In the next chapter, "Rehearse, Rehearse, Rehearse," my friend David Smith offers wisdom about the best way to learn by doing.

Equipping
Role-Playing, by David Smith

When I was very young, I was extremely shy. I would hide behind my mother's skirt, and I would turn brilliant red under the bright lights of the least amount of attention by strangers or adults.

In my first performance on stage while in the third grade, I was called upon to play the dignified Governor Bradford. I had only one brief line to speak. We had practiced that line in the classroom several times. As the hour approached, we stood off-stage, listening to the audience talking to each other, jostling for their seats. One person coughed, then another, then more shuffling. The room was filled with senior citizens, my school friends, and their parents. The moment had arrived, the teacher announced the program was going to begin. I was nervous, but also excited to play such an important role.

I strode out across the stage in my stately Governors robe. The robe was a little long for my third-grade legs. Before I could say a word, while I was still in motion, I tripped and fell face-down, sprawled across the stage. The entire room burst into laughter. I was mortified. I felt the clumsy oaf, struggling to get back on my feet amidst the laughter, with all those eyes staring at me! My vision began to blur as my tear ducts refused to remain inactive. I was flushed. I could feel my ears burning. All I could think of was, "how can I get out of here?"

Many Christians have experienced the feeling of tripping over themselves. They may know the same flashes of heat and the burning of ears, as they recall previous attempts to "evangelize" at school or work. You might feel the heat just anticipating the possibility of sharing your faith.

Most of us enjoy watching a skilled actor or actress in a play or movie. In the same way, we admire a gifted evangelist when we see them in action. But in both cases, we could never see ourselves stepping into their shoes and making a go of it.

How does one become an actor?

We might say, "they are gifted." That is true, but were they always as gifted as they are now? What about acting classes? Rehearsals? Small parts? Tryouts?

Coaches in the Church

What would happen if we could find a way for apostles, prophets, evangelists, pastors, and teachers to function like acting coaches, "equipping the saints" to be able to tell their story of faith effectively? We might see the average "saint" speak out boldly, telling their friends and neighbors a compelling story of how they encountered God.

What if we could find time to run one of our church meetings like a sales training meeting? For those of you who have never been to a sales meeting, they like to do an exercise called "role-playing." Role-playing is where every person takes their turn to practice what they would say and do as they try to "convince a co-worker" to buy the product.

We pretend (like acting) to convince a "brother salesperson" about our experience with the product. They make up questions (they already know the answers to) and we practice providing the answers (they

Equipping

already know). The bottom line – it is a safe place to make mistakes and to learn how to avoid them.

The sales manager is there to observe and comment. But then the rest of the team (sales guys) provide insight and suggestions on how to make our message clearer.

This practice offers a better understanding of how the evangelist could equip the saints to do the work of evangelistic ministry. Role-playing takes away the fear of the unknown. Because we have already experienced it in role-playing, it is no longer unknown.

It took me ten years to get up the courage to get back on the stage. In high school, I tried out for the play my senior year. It was my last chance, and I was surprised when I was chosen for the lead role. This time I had over three hundred lines to memorize in a long three-act play.

That play ended up running several weeks beyond the original school play weekend. I able to face the crowd and even play the crowd a bit, as I got more comfortable being "in character." How did this happen?

I had discovered my new identity. I was now "Robert." In the role of Robert, I was no longer a shy young man. How did I get to that place of being able to speak with confidence, after being in the place of being too shy to speak at all?

Rehearse

Rehearse, rehearse, rehearse. I rehearsed those lines for weeks. At first, I practiced alone, reading them over and over out loud. Then I practiced with my parents and

Role-Playing, by David Smith

with other characters in the rehearsals at school. All rehearsals are really role-playing. They involve reading the lines, playing with the lines, using different body language to convey emotion, always being coached along the way. The director said, "try this" or "try walking over here and pause" or "turn half-way round before you deliver that line." The coaching, the practice, the repeating of the lines, all built to the excitement of the dress rehearsal.

It was the lack of the dress rehearsal that caused my downfall in third grade. If I had practiced walking out in that robe on that platform at a dress rehearsal, I might have delivered my line and saved a myself a ten-year sabbatical.

Sadly, most Christians cannot say they have had a coach to help block their steps or rehearse their lines. In our gatherings, do we equip the saints to tell their story of faith (their testimony)?

What if we realized that the church can learn from a sales organization? In a sales organization, the "senior leader" is a sales manager. In my 28 years of experience in sales organizations, I have a love/hate relationship with role-playing. I hate the awkward process of trying to pretend a role-playing mate is a prospect. They know where I am going, and they know the answers, but are acting as though they don't. I don't like to play the games. In the game of pretending to sell a concept or idea, the role-playing mate always asks a more difficult question than you would ever get in the marketplace.

On the other hand, I love role-playing for one reason. Once I get past the awkward, embarrassing part, I

Equipping

am pretty good at turning a phrase or discovering creative ways to show how the product is the perfect solution. I love hearing the other players walk through their scenes. I learn new ways to answer objections by watching them struggle through during rehearsal (role-playing) of their lines. When they discover a new way to communicate more clearly than ever before, the whole room realizes what just happened. An average man or woman has been equipped to evangelize.

What if we saw discipleship as teaching others to tell their story in a more clear and effective way? Role-playing is a "dress rehearsal" of sorts. You can rewrite the lines as you step out in faith, sharing your story with "friends" and "family" in your local gathering.

A "dress rehearsal" includes how it sounds when you say it out loud, answering questions that come up as you share your story of faith.

Go ahead, brother, "break a leg."

The Discerning Heart, by David Smith

We have considered the value of role-playing. Could we do role-playing in our church services? Would you believe that Paul promotes role-playing in every church service? Paul taught the Corinthian church that church services should incorporate role-playing by every member in every service. It sounds like a sales training meeting where everyone gets to role-play. Let's read it.

> *How is it then, brethren? Whenever you come together, each of you has a psalm, has a teaching, has a tongue, has a revelation, has an interpretation. Let all things be done for edification. 1 Corinthians 14:26 (NKJV)*

In the first line, Apostle Paul promotes role-playing in every church service.

When? Whenever!

"*How is it then, brethren?* **Whenever** *you come together.*" The word "whenever" includes all gatherings. In other words, it means every service, every time, both formal and informal gatherings, smaller and larger gatherings.

Who? Everyone!

"*...****each of you*** *has a psalm, has a teaching, has a tongue, has a revelation, has an interpretation.*"

How many should we allow? All of them!

Why? For edification!

"*Let all things be done for* ***edification.***"

Equipping

If we were rehearsing for a play, how many scenes should we rehearse?

"All of them" is the right answer.

How many actors should rehearse their lines?

"All of them" again is the correct answer.

Handling Prophecies

Then Paul gives further instructions on the "how to" of coaching the saints to bring forth and handle the prophecies God gives them. I personally do not know of any church today that is following this pattern given by Paul.

> *Let two or three prophets speak, and let the others judge. But if anything is revealed to another who sits by, let the first keep silent. For you can all prophesy one by one, that all may learn and all may be encouraged. 1 Corinthians 14:29-31 (NKJV)*

Notice that "speak" is first, and "judge" is second.

Most churches which allow prophecy at all use a two-step process. First, the word is judged privately by bringing it to the leader. Second, if the word is approved, it can be delivered publicly. This is a convenient method for leaders to keep a service moving efficiently. But it circumvents a critical learning experience for equipping the saints, both the speakers and the hearers. "Equipping the saints" is a mandate for leaders, especially five-fold leaders.

In the end, the result of this convenient method is that we keep the saints immature in their discernment.

We keep them from being tested as a discerning "hearer" or speaker.

Because we choose to judge the word privately (off microphone) and disallow any word that is not 100% clean, the saints never get a chance to discern prophecy.

If we could handle the inconvenience and allow the speaker to speak first, we could have the hearers assess the word themselves. Then afterward (this passage says after two or three prophecies), a leader could judge the words. For the hearers, this would either confirm their growing ability to discern the voice of God or correct their assessment. In this way, the saints would hone their ability to hear and judge for themselves. It also allows the speaker to learn when he hears correctly from God.

It has been said, "If you give a man a fish he eats for one day, but if you teach him to fish you feed him for a lifetime."

What if we changed that just a bit.

If you give the saints a "pre-cleaned" word, they will eat for that day. But if you teach them how to catch and "clean" a word, you will teach them how to eat (discern) for a lifetime.

When we advocate role-playing in every service, as part of discipleship, then the pattern becomes critical for raising up discerning prophets and saints.

Discernment for Eternity

Let's look ahead, down the road. Did you know our destiny is not just to get to heaven sit down and play our harp? Instead, it is to rule and reign with Christ.

Equipping

I asked a friend this question. "What if tomorrow morning a long black limousine pulled up to your door? The presidential seal and the national flag are flying from the corners of the front bumper. Secret service agents knock on your door and announce to you, 'You are now acting president of the United States of America. You are needed in the situation room immediately for a matter of international impact.' As they escort you to the car and as you ride off in the back of that limo to travel to the White House, what would you be wishing you had spent more time studying? A new language? American history? A course of law? Domestic issues? Foreign cultures?"

You see, someday that is going to happen to all the saints. Jesus said, "I am coming again." He is coming for a bride who will rule nations with him. The scriptures also tell us we are going to judge angels. What are you doing to gain an understanding heart?

Solomon asked this.

> *Therefore give to Your servant an understanding heart to judge Your people, that I may discern between good and evil. For who is able to judge this great people of Yours?" 1 Kings 3:9 (NKJV)*

Where are the saints going to gain (by practice) that discerning heart?

Going

This section recalls what the leaders of the early church did to fulfill the Great Commission. In this context, we will examine contemporary efforts to take the gospel to the world.

The Great Commission

My wife and I have always liked to travel. Thus far I have visited 47 of the 50 states in the US plus 8 of 10 provinces in Canada.

In 2009, we bought a small travel trailer. We wanted to tour the western United States, weighing options for moving west as we approached what is the normal retirement age.

We like to go places.

At the end of his ministry on earth, Jesus told the disciples to go places.

> *Jesus came and told his disciples, "I have been given all authority in heaven and on earth. Therefore, go and make disciples of all the nations, baptizing them in the name of the Father and the Son and the Holy Spirit. Teach these new disciples to obey all the commands I have given you. And be sure of this: I am with you always, even to the end of the age." Matthew 28:18-20 (NLT)*

You can interpret the "go" part of this commission as a continuous action, literally "going." In English, we

Going

would say "As you go..." This is a good understanding. We should be ready to share our faith anytime, anywhere. You could say 24-7-365. Twenty-four hours a day, seven days a week, 365 days a year.

But "go" is best understood as a command to start doing something we weren't doing before. Jesus told the disciples to go to "all nations," which was much further than before. We too should understand the Great Commission as a command to us, to start going and continue going to places we haven't been before.

The church does some of this. Virtually all denominations and many local churches support missionaries, both domestic and foreign. Some Christians feel called by God to go out as missionaries. Many of us have the perspective that some folks go out as missionaries while the rest of us stay home and support them with prayer and finances.

Supporting our missionaries is good. But the reality in America is that the church is losing influence. Many people have become disillusioned with church and stopped attending. We have in this country a large mission field. Who are the missionaries? God would say every believer is a missionary.

This is how it was at the beginning of church history. Consider what happens in Act, several years after the launch of the church at Pentecost.

> *But the believers who were scattered preached the Good News about Jesus wherever they went. Acts 8:4 (NLT)*

The Great Commission

Meanwhile, the believers who had been scattered during the persecution after Stephen's death traveled as far as Phoenicia, Cyprus, and Antioch of Syria. They preached the word of God, but only to Jews. However, some of the believers who went to Antioch from Cyprus and Cyrene began preaching to the Gentiles about the Lord Jesus. The power of the Lord was with them, and a large number of these Gentiles believed and turned to the Lord. Acts 11:19-21 (NLT)

Christians will always gather in community. That is where we experience worship, teaching, fellowship, and prayer. These are the basic features of church life. Jesus told us church "happens" where two or three gather.

Too often we see the boundaries of the church as the walls of the building. Yes, some churches undertake outreach efforts, offering clothing or food to needy people in the community. Such efforts are commendable and sometimes lead to a God encounter for the one being served.

Jesus told us to pray for workers to bring in the harvest. What if every believer approached their place in the community as a mission field? This does not mean handing out tracts to everyone at the office, factory, or school, although we should be a "living tract." It means is that we look to the Holy Spirit to give us opportunities to be "salt and light" in the world.

This might involve offering a smile, a hug, or a short word of counsel to someone with a problem. This word

Going

of counsel can be, "this has been my experience," with or without a verse of scripture.

Being salt and light might involve more than a smile, such as praying for someone in need. Holy Spirit will prepare you for and arrange such encounters.

These kinds of encounters are the essence of being missions-minded. Every believer has a sphere of influence – people who know us, respect us, and will listen to us. We don't need to preach a sermon. We do need to be ready to witness to what Jesus has done in our lives. That's all.

Every local church should encourage every believer to go places and tell others about Jesus. This means more than an occasional motivational message about what we "should" do. Each believer should come to the place where they think in their heart that they are able to tell others about Jesus. Then they can learn to recognize and respond to opportunities. It will help to hear testimonies, stories from people who have spoken to others in the marketplace. Role plays may help, giving believers practical experience about how to steer a conversation towards matters of faith. We explored some of these ideas in the chapters on Equipping.

Sharing Our Faith

As a teenage Christian, I experimented with witnessing to others about my faith. I will always remember a visit one evening to Kent State University, near where I lived in Ohio. I went with a friend. We split up at the Student Union, each of us with a fistful of tracts published by Campus Crusade for Christ. I initiated conversations with a few students, sharing the *Four Spiritual Laws* tract. I don't remember now if anyone "prayed the prayer" with me.

Some years later I found myself on the streets of Minneapolis, in a couple of downtown locations, doing the same thing. We initiated conversations in the hope of "leading someone to Christ." Again, I don't recall a significant positive response. God knows.

God does gift some of his people as evangelists. For a few years, I was part of a jail ministry team. Our group included a "mom" (with a shepherd's heart), a couple of teachers, and a guy that was unmistakably gifted as an evangelist. He would make an appeal at the right time with the right words, and people responded with a commitment to Jesus.

All Christians are candidates for sharing their faith from time to time. In Acts, when persecution scattered the people, they went everywhere giving witness to Jesus (Acts 8:4).

Going

Marketplace Ministry

In the contemporary church, there is a great divide between "ordained" ministers and "lay" members. I tackle this theme in the chapter, "Ministry Positions." My dad was a full-time pastor, but I chose to enter the so-called secular workplace. After ten years in my chosen profession, I recommitted my life to Jesus. Then I began to soak in the Bible, read devotional books, get involved in church, and attend conferences. These are all typical activities for a committed Christian, and God taught me many lessons.

But there was more to learn. God led me to start a business, even though that was not part of my education or skillset. God used the business to teach me basic lessons of faith. We saw God intervene supernaturally in difficult situations. A couple of times we were down to our last two dollars, and we saw God prove himself faithful.

And then during a quiet time one day, God made my priorities clear. The business was not only about having a job or supporting my family, although those were important. Rather, God gave me the business to teach me lessons about himself, about life, about people, and about ministry. I could have learned many of these lessons in full-time ministry. But they could be learned as well in the workplace.

God reinforced this message through a couple of powerful prophetic words. He said that my life is to be given to building the church, not building a business. The business was a means to an end. I'm not saying this

Marketplace Ministry

is a lesson for every Christian businessman, but it was a lesson for me, and maybe for others.

In the late 1990s, my wife and I engaged with *Lighthouses of Prayer*, a ministry led by Ed Silvoso and his associates. Silvoso wrote books and created videos supporting his message of Christians taking their faith to the marketplace – everywhere they shop, work, or otherwise interact with people. This ministry introduced us to the idea of "friendship evangelism." This involved a prayer-care-share pattern of approaching people. In this model, you begin by praying from a distance. At some point, you show caring for the person, their family, and their needs. In time, you may have an opportunity to talk to them about Jesus. We felt this approach was better than the tracts-on-the-street model, at least for us. In many ways, this is still our way of approaching people about Jesus. The key to this approach is to truly care about people. They know when you're looking for another "notch in your belt."

About this same time, in 2002, we expanded our small software business by adding four employees to the two we had. When we first started the business in the mid-1980s, we intended to serve the Lord in any way we could. We hired our first employee in the mid-1990s. When decisions about pay and other concerns came up, we looked to the advice offered by Larry Burkett through his ministry, Christian Financial Concepts.

One of the employees we hired in 2002 encouraged me to write out a statement of vision and values for the company. This I did, making it clear that our goal was to serve God in what we did. In our published

Going

statement, we committed to look to God for guidance in company decisions.

This brought us squarely into the marketplace ministry world. We have continued to see the business as a vehicle for ministry, partly because of the product we built. Our charting software for public health nurses serves "the least of these" in our communities. Many of the clients of our customers are elderly women or young single mothers.

As the years have passed, God has brought us new resources on the topic of marketplace ministry. In 2009, we met with John Garfield, who encouraged us in several ways. We began to see that could be effective ministers even though we held jobs in the marketplace rather than in the church.

We recommend this book for more information on marketplace ministry:

Releasing Kings for Ministry in the Marketplace, by Harold Eberle and John Garfield

Seven Mountains

In the early 2000s, we encountered the Seven Mountains message. This movement began with a supernatural, God-arranged meeting between Loren Cunningham, leader of Youth with a Mission, and Bill Bright, leader of Campus Crusade for Christ (www.7culturalmountains.org). Our home group studied a video series by Lance Wallnau on Seven Mountains. This message says that God has believers in seven different places of influence in modern culture: government, church, education, family, media, arts, and business. This message also says that all Christians have a ministry outside the church, in one of these "marketplace" venues.

Some have criticized this idea as suggesting that the church "takes over" the world through these spheres of influence. Such a view is called dominion theology. This is not the way we understand the Seven Mountains message. In our view, this teaching encourages Christians to influence the world wherever they live. Many Christians live a life in Christ on Sunday mornings in the church building, and perhaps an occasional hour during the week. The core of the Seven Mountains message is to live as a Christian 24/7/265 – everywhere we go, all the time. Jesus said we are to be salt and light to the world (Matthew 5:13-16). For us, this teaching was an encouragement to go places and share our faith, according to the Great Commission.

Going

Come In or Go Out?

Life is a succession of choices about coming and going. We "go" to school or work or to visit a friend. Afterwards we "come" home. Home is the place of warmth and friendship and family. Going is the place of adventure and reward, whether we are a 7-year old playing with friends or a 37-year old building a career. Obviously, this is simplistic. Many women build a career in the home, caring for their family.

Many regard the church as a family, and many scriptures use the language of family. We are sons and daughters of our Father. We regard each other as brothers and sisters in the Lord. When we gather together in a church building, it's easy to think of it as our church "home."

In today's church, the primary message is "come in." Church members are encouraged to invite friends to the church meeting. Some churches have adopted a "seeker sensitive" strategy, using coffee in the lobby and other methods to appeal to visitors. Other churches use a variety of outreach methods to serve their community. They do this with a heart to serve those in need, but also in the hope that some of those served will "come in" to the local church.

In the chapter, "The Great Commission," we looked at the command of Jesus to "go out." This often takes the form of giving to missions or community outreach activities. It might also include encouraging each person in the local church to reach out in their sphere of influence to touch others for Christ. This might involve praying for people, sharing a witness, and more. I explored these possibilities in the chapter, "Sharing Our Faith."

What is the balance between coming in and going out? Even in the churches most oriented to going-out, the balance of effort is probably 80-20 in favor of coming in. What should it be?

The Early Church

Let's look to the Bible for guidance on this question. The early church grew by leaps and bounds, partly because meetings were public, in the temple. It also seems likely that people were being invited into homes for fellowship and meals. I explore patterns in the early church in the chapter, "The Acts 2 Lifestyle." Is it possible the church had a 50-50 mix of "coming in" and "going out" at that time? It seems reasonable that the teaching of the apostles in the temple and the signs and wonders in the streets represented "going out." This contrasted with sharing meals and fellowship represented "coming in." This seems like a good balance. Today, teaching would be done both in the church building and in homes or other locations.

When Saul started persecuting the church, the believers were scattered. As they went, they carried the gospel message with them. It is possible that for a time the balance in the church was weighted toward "going out." In time, as new churches were established, the balance probably returned to a more equal mix of coming in and going out.

Going

As we read the account of Paul's journeys in the Acts, the focus is on the going out. But we know that at the same time as Paul was going out, the believers in Antioch continued to function as a local church. We know the church in Antioch met in many locations in the city. Their activities would have been like those in Jerusalem described in Acts 2 and Acts 4.

The Modern Church

Some might say the modern church has a correct balance, given the thousands of missionaries that serve at home and overseas. In my view, given the general decline of the church in America, we have lost the proper balance. As stated earlier, the typical American church says, "come in."

In looking for an explanation, we can say that modern life emphasizes comfort. This is not true for major segments of society, those who experience poverty and injustice. But the ingenuity and productivity of American business have made life at home comfortable for the majority. The typical sermon seldom challenges this preference for comfort which is common to us all.

Equipping Gifts

Another factor contributing to this pattern is that most church meetings are led by a someone with a pastoral gift. We looked at the Ephesians 4 equipping gifts in the chapter, "Five Equipping Gifts."

Some of these five gifts are oriented to believers and the "come in" message. Pastors and teachers are gifted to feed and nurture the people in the church. These roles

Come In or Go Out?

are assigned to create the church "home." As such, their natural orientation is a "come in" message.

The gifts of prophet and evangelist can function in both capacities. Prophets will often give direction and correction to the church. But it is also true that God will often pair an apostle and a prophet in an assignment to "go out." God did this with Paul and Silas.

The evangelist may share the gospel in a local church meeting, perhaps as a visiting speaker. Some will find salvation in this way. A church led by a fivefold evangelist will grow. These kinds of evangelists support a "come in" message. But evangelists may also take the gospel to new territories, perhaps as a missionary. Such an assignment is a "go out" message, although in time new churches will be formed, often turned over to a pastoral leader.

This leaves the apostolic gift, which is oriented to a "go out" message.

Thus, two of these fivefold gifts, evangelists and apostles, have the role of equipping believers to "go out." If churches are neglecting the assignment of going out, then we may be giving too little credence to the roles of evangelist and apostle in the contemporary church.

21st Century Church

In this section, we consider what it is like for someone to work out a meaningful church life. We explore finding a balance between new ideas and church traditions.

Assembling the Puzzle

For many years, one of our daughters loved to assemble picture puzzles. She was very good at it, from a young age. Eventually, we tackled a 5,000-piece puzzle, and I could tell her interest was waning when I found myself doing most of the puzzle.

When we try to assemble a picture of what church should look like, we face the same challenge. We see a picture in the Bible of a dynamic, effective church, in Antioch or Ephesus (keeping in mind that no church is perfect). But as we look at the puzzle pieces in our current situation, the ones "in our hands," we often struggle to put the pieces together. We assemble a few pieces at the edges – love God, love others. But when we get into the center of the puzzle it gets more difficult.

God helps us. He walks with us through experiences designed to shape our attitudes, our behavior, our beliefs, our relationships. Along the way, we have experiences which teach us both what is good and what is bad for us. Like a good parent, our Father will "train a child in the way in which he should go, and when he is older, he will not depart from it."

Assembling the Puzzle

Many of us grew up in church, and as children, we learned what taught, either by words or actions. As adults, we sometimes need to unlearn some of what we learned as children. God helps us with this. At one point, I bought a well-known study Bible with extensive marginal notes. At the time, I was pursuing discipleship, and as I studied scripture, I also absorbed ideas from the notes. After a year or so, I began to hear Holy Spirit say to my spirit, "that's not quite right." Sometimes I even heard Holy Spirit say, "that's not even close." Over time, I realized a significant percentage of the marginal notes were off-base, and after a few years of diligent study in that Bible, I set it aside. I still have that bible. It reminds me of a time when I was soaking in the scriptures, using markers to high-light hundreds of meaningful verses. God taught me an important lesson – to interpret scripture by the Spirit.

21st Century Church
Remaining Teachable

As we grow in the Lord, we often need to leave behind ideas we learned earlier in life. In my experience, God regularly brings me books or messages or experiences I need. Each one is designed to teach me what I need to know at this precise point on the journey of my life. I explore this theme in the chapter, "The School of Christ." When I get a new book, I read it with a highlighter. When I am finished, I go back and transcribe the highlights of the highlights into an electronic document, with page number references to the book. Then I print these in a half-page format that fits into my journal. Often, I return later to review the highlights. These electronic documents are also easy to search. I can go back and find an idea I know I read "somewhere."

As I learn new ideas, I am sometimes forced to leave behind old ideas. For me, it's a matter of evaluating whether the new idea "fits the puzzle" of my faith. I find it challenging to hold two opposing views of thought, although sometimes the Bible does expect us to do that – to hold, at the same time, two seemingly opposing ideas. One example of two apparently opposing ideas is God's sovereignty and man's responsibility, both of which are true. For me, adopting a new idea may require abandoning an old idea. I expect this pattern to continue for the rest of my life.

Some of the ideas my wife and I needed to unlearn were doctrines and beliefs. In our case, we had to unlearn the idea that our identity is "sinner." This idea is foundational to liturgies in many churches, including the mainline church we attended for a decade in our thirties. But the Bible calls us a new creation (2 Corinthians 5:17), a saint (1 Corinthians 1:2), with the mind of Christ (1 Corinthians 2:16). What do we believe? Do we believe a doctrine handed down through centuries of church history, or do we believe the words of scripture? In time, we chose to believe our identity is that of saints, not sinners. This change revolutionized our faith, and made us far more able to resist the criticism we received from many in the church.

Not all the ideas we unlearned were beliefs. Some of them were church practices. God brought us books and messages that challenged some of the ways we do church in contemporary America. Not all the new ideas were right for us. Some authors and speakers were working out of a need to "resist" authority. Others were speaking out of a need to exert control over others. It can be difficult to sort out these diverse and often conflicting ideas, especially if you want to be a good Berean, searching the scriptures to "see if these things be so" (Acts 17:11).

21st Century Church
Finding Truth

Finding truth can be difficult. Sometimes you learn by experience – trying different ideas and assessing the fruit. Sometimes you learn by revelation – hearing God tell you which way to go.

Some Christians would say, just go by the Bible. This is good advice. But the more I studied the scriptures, the more I realized that many verses in scripture are open to multiple understandings. It seemed to depend on the doctrinal background of the reader. How else can we have some Christians holding to a literal millennium, and others to a figurative millennium? How else can we have division among about when Christ returns, either before or after a "great tribulation"?

About fifteen years into "searching the scriptures," I picked up and read a popular systematic theology by Wayne Grudem. Dr. Grudem provides an appendix in many chapters, citing alternative understandings of the topic under discussion. Various scriptures support each point of view.

How easy it would be to grow up in a local church that is part of a denomination and never wrestle with which doctrines and beliefs are right and which might be somewhat off. That was never going to work for me. I was the son of a Presbyterian pastor and baptized as an infant. At the age of confirmation (8th grade for me), my dad was a chaplain in the Navy, and he put me in a local Methodist church for confirmation class. A year

Finding Truth

later we moved to California where I attended a Southern Baptist church. During their summer camp, I responded to an altar call for salvation.

In college, my wife and I enjoyed services at the campus Episcopal chapel. After college, we were living in Minnesota, where most people are Catholic or Lutheran. We attended the neighborhood Lutheran Church. How could I follow the steps of my youth, when I had been involved in four major Protestant denominations, with different beliefs and practices? I couldn't. I needed to embark on a path to find the truth for myself.

I am not saying that every person has their own "personal" truth. Rather, once you have decided that no one denomination and no one pastor has everything right, you must sort out what to believe and what to practice. That's what we did. We learned to trust scripture, revelation, experience, discussions with other believers, and God.

21st Century Church

The Acts 2 Lifestyle

The early church was different from today's church in several ways. Many Christians who become frustrated with their local church look back at the early church. They think that if we follow the pattern of Acts, we will do better. Perhaps.

But, God promises in Isaiah 41:19-20 to do a "new thing," which may not match up exactly to either the past or the present way of doing church. Otherwise, it would not be new.

We know that the outworking of the gospel often leads to new patterns. Jesus tells us in John 3:8 that the "Spirit blows where it will."

Even so, let's look at the patterns of the early church, to see what we can glean for today.

We find a summary of the early church pattern in Acts 2, not long after Pentecost.

> *They committed themselves to the teaching of the apostles, the life together, the common meal, and the prayers. Acts 2:42 (MSG)*

> *All the believers devoted themselves to the apostles' teaching, and to fellowship, and to sharing in meals (including the Lord's Supper), and to prayer. Acts 2:42 (NLT)*

Today, the Sunday morning gathering focuses on worship and preaching. In the past, many churches also held meetings on Sunday evening and Wednesday

The Acts 2 Lifestyle

evening. These gave an opportunity for prayer, fellowship, and in-depth teaching. Because attendance at these "extra" meeting times declined over the years, few churches still offer them. Today, in a typical week, the believer enjoys a half-hour of worship plus a half-hour sermon from the pulpit.

When we compare this to the Acts 2 lifestyle, there are a few missing ingredients. Yes, churches still offer opportunities for fellowship, shared meals, and prayer. These may involve an additional hour a week, for a small percentage of the church. But something is missing.

In the early church, there was ample demonstration, discussion, and learning by doing. People saw the gospel acted out in community by other believers. As they gathered in fellowship and over meals, they discussed the gospel and what God was doing in their midst. They were doing what they heard taught by the apostles. Some of this is clear in the verses we read in Acts. In other cases, you must read between the lines. But it's there.

How might our gatherings change if we followed the Acts 2 pattern? Do we need to make more room for the "life together" and "sharing in meals"? Do we want our formal meetings to now and then offer demonstration and discussion?

Many churches have a "pot blessing" meal from time to time, which of course includes fellowship. But what would it look like to make these activities frequent and the focus of gatherings?

21st Century Church

The Alpha Course, a discussion-style study of the basics of Christian faith, does this. Their format is a meal plus fellowship plus discussion-style teaching. Many churches offer an Alpha Course group as an event in the calendar of church life. But seldom is the format a primary pattern of a local church.

Alpha Course targets non-believers or young Christians. What would a variation of the format look like for a typical church member who is learning and growing beyond the basics?

What About Church Traditions?

You've heard the joke. Propose a change in the local church setting, and you'll hear a reply defending the status quo, "But we've always done it that way."

This is not true everywhere. We visited a church in Seattle that, in the face of declining attendance, moved into several locations in the community to offer dinner along with worship and a gospel message to homeless folks and others (www.communitydinners.com). One church in Portland meets in a ballroom above a non-profit pub, and uses the proceeds of the pub to fund community service projects (www.theoregoncommunity.com).

These churches have gone far outside the box of church convention. Whatever you think of beer in a church setting, these churches are reaching people for Jesus that would not otherwise be reached.

When I use the term church traditions, I speak of "the way we do church." This includes many factors. Some are specific to the meeting: the order of service, the arrangement of chairs, the style of music, leadership of the meeting. Other factors include the way decisions are made, the type of buildings used for meetings, and more.

A study of church history shows that many of our church traditions go back centuries. Many go back to the beginning of the denomination associated with our local church. If your church is Baptist, Episcopal, Lutheran, Methodist, or Presbyterian, much of how you do church

21st Century Church

goes back to the 1500s or 1700s. If your church is Roman Catholic or Orthodox, your traditions go back further.

Most denominations have a few traditions going back to the 300s AD, when Christianity became the official religion of Rome. These common traditions include a service led by one or two people, a sermon spoken from a pulpit, and people sitting in rows to hear the sermon.

What about non-denominational churches? They tend to have many of the same traditions as denominations, but with an emphasis on local governance.

Some churches, both denominational and non-denominational, have stepped away from church traditions. Such churches may permit several people to speak, or they may arrange chairs in a circle or at tables.

In our experience, we have seen at least three perspectives people take toward religious traditions. There are some who find great comfort in traditions. In the extreme, this point of view can oppose a change in the color of the carpet.

There are some who want nothing to do with church traditions. They may point out that some of the ways we "do church" originated with Roman government or modern business practices. Some may avoid attending a local church, stating as a reason their opposition to "one man in charge" and other traditions.

We find ourselves somewhere in the middle. We want to honor traditions that bless others, and which are foundational to most churches. At the same time, we see great benefit in many of the changes we see in the 21st century.

Finding Church

For my wife and I, the puzzle of church life is coming together. Every person must sort out what to do with new patterns of belief and practice. Perhaps your local church does not teach Father's love, the identity of the believer, or grace. Your local church may not offer opportunities for new ways of gathering, equipping, or going. In the third part of this book, "Rivers in Your Life," we will offer ideas for someone in this situation.

There are many ways to experience new themes of belief and practice. Over time, we have learned what kind of church experience we want. Our goal has been to experience God. We want to do this in fellowship with others who are earnestly pursuing God. This includes prayer, worship, study, and service to others.

This has led us to certain preferences. Everyone has preferences. These are ours. In every case, although we see value in the second pattern, on the right, we prefer the first pattern, on the left.

We value contemporary worship over
traditional choruses and hymns.

We value prayer with a group of friends over
structured prayer meetings.

We value teachings that challenge us over
"preaching to the choir" messages.

We value spontaneous ministry over
structured outreach events.

Even though we have these preferences, we find it easy to participate in church meetings that do not support these preferences. By this, I mean we can happily be part of a traditional church service when it serves the purposes of God in supporting others in what they do.

We recommend these books for more information on Finding Church.

So You Don't Want to Go to Church Anymore, by Jake Colsen

Finding Church, by Wayne Jacobsen

Part Two
Rivers in My Life

Early Days

This section brings a personal dimension to rivers of life in the church. I encountered new ways of gathering and equipping early in my walk with God.

Personal Revival

Although I have long been fascinated by revivals in church history, it all starts with personal revival. My personal revival has roots in in my teenage years, with an altar call experience at summer camp. Twenty years later I had become weary of church-as-usual, looking for something more meaningful. A friend invited me on a 2,000-mile road trip – Minnesota to Oklahoma and back. Along the way, we spent a day with a friend of his that wanted little to do with church but much to do with Jesus. His name was Lyle, and he is one of four people I name in the dedication to this book. I came away from that trip determined to pursue Jesus, resulting in a decision to read my Bible cover-to-cover. Two years later I prayed for the baptism of the Holy Spirit, using a booklet my dad had given me years before. Thus began a personal revival which has continued for over thirty years.

Any Christian bookstore will have many books on this subject. Some focus on intimacy with God, or approaches to reading the Bible, or hearing God's voice. Anyone who pursues God for a time will learn what is

Personal Revival

needful to learn. Holy Spirit, our Teacher, desires nothing more than for each of us to encounter Jesus and Father in a personal and powerful way.

A key practice for me was to start the day with God. This involved, for me as for many others, time spent in reading, praying, and worship. My hunger was such that my "quiet times" grew to an hour, then to two hours, and for a time, even longer. This pattern of an early hour was reinforced by having children in the house – eventually six. With a large family, the only part of the day that permits a *quiet* time is either very early, before rising for school and work, or at the end of the day, after the kids are in bed. In my case, I was so tired at the end of the day that only the morning would work. And it did. Most of my early growth as a committed Christian resulted from my morning times with God. This included time spent with great men of God, through their books and audio messages.

Pursuing More

After fifteen years of personal revival, I found myself on a flight across the Pacific as part of a mission trip to the Philippines. Sitting beside the pastor of our church, I asked what to pursue next in my faith walk. He recommended a practice which had been helpful for him – going away for a weekend retreat with one's wife, for reflection, prayer, conversation, and study. I began to do this, and was blessed to find a retreat facility on a lake near my home. They had built a small cabin called a hermitage, about 12 feet by 12 feet square. In time, they build a larger hermitage with a double bed, and my wife

Early Days

joined me. These were wonderful, powerful times of experiencing and growing closer to God.

A life of personal revival is difficult in modern America. We are too busy. I found it easier because I was self-employed, and could choose to go to work later than others. But everyone has 168 hours in a week. At one point, I decided to do a tally of how many discretionary hours I had in my week, and was astonished. For me, discretionary time was what was left over after sleeping, eating, personal care, errands, school, work, and church meetings. Even though I had a 40-hour work week, I still had well over 20 hours of discretionary time in my week. It broke down as a couple of hours each evening, plus several hours on Saturday and most of Sunday. The question is, how do we spend our discretionary time? A significant share of that needs to be spent with family and friends. But some of it is well spent with God. A life of personal revival seems to require a commitment of time.

I am convinced that personal revival is a key stepping-stone to corporate revival – revival in the church. God is looking for a core of committed Christians who are walking in profound personal revival. This was the foundation for the early church, and it is still a pattern for today.

A Cave of Adullam

As a young child I enjoyed living in a cave. Of course, my cave consisted of a blanket thrown over a card table or a corner of a closet with the door closed. I furnished my cave with a light in the corner, along with a book and a pillow, and a snack if Mom permitted.

Eventually, I outgrew cave-life. Then at age 37, a friend who had begun to disciple me told me I was called to the Cave of Adullam, to be part of "David's company." I had little understanding of what that meant, but in the thirty years since then, I have come to appreciate what he meant. If you have read this far, you too may be called to the Cave of Adullam.

We encounter this Cave of Adullam in David's life when he was fleeing from Saul. Before long 400 men joined him from various places in Israel.

> *All those who were in distress or in debt or discontented gathered around him, and he became their leader. About four hundred men were with him. 1 Samuel 22:2 (NIV)*

If you walk into a Christian bookstore today, looking for wisdom on how to build your church, you will not be urged to appeal to malcontents. Most churches have too many of those already, right? Yet this is what God did as the word got out that David was hiding from Saul. These malcontents had heard of David's exploits in the contest with Goliath. But with Saul threatening to

Early Days

kill David, they were taking a big risk to join David in the Cave. And David was taking a risk to let them in.

But God had a plan. As these men walked with David, they were transformed. They fought with David, and became warriors like David. The exploits of these men are celebrated in 2 Samuel 23. Moreover, as these men lived with David they became devoted to God like David. They watched God come and win battles for them (1 Samuel 23:4 and 30:23). They watched David refuse to kill Saul when it would have been easy (1 Samuel 24:7 and 26:9). We can imagine that many of them served as officials in the government of Israel after David became king.

Can you imagine what life was like for David's men in the Cave? It would have been nothing like my cozy childhood cave. These guys were on the run, carrying little more than minimal food and clothing. Today we call this "subsistence" living, a lifestyle chosen by very few.

Life in a Cave of Adullam Today

Let's revisit the word of the Lord given to me 30 years ago. As I look back, I see many lessons at the hand of God designed to bring me to my destiny. Many of these are difficult lessons, even unpleasant lessons, like those experienced by David's men in the Cave of Adullam. Here are some of the lessons along the way.

- **Commitment**. Will you pursue God on your own, beyond commitments to church meetings?

- **Obedience**. How do you respond when God asks you to do a hard thing?
- **Mentors**. Will you seek out those who would be good mentors for you? A good mentor will suggest ways to pursue God, encourage you along the way, and hold you accountable.
- **Authority**. How do you respond when a person of spiritual authority says or does something you don't like? (Note: There must be a balance between honoring a person in authority and being obedient to God. See Acts 4:19, where Peter and John stand before the Jewish council. This principle must be pursued in prayer.)
- **Relationship**. How will you respond when God asks you to be close to people who are different from you, or even people who are disagreeable?
- **Conflict**. How will you respond when you find yourself in conflict with another believer, possibly a leader? Will you be offended and walk away? Will you be open to forgiveness and reconciliation?
- **Warfare**. Will you learn to identify what the enemy of your soul is doing in your life, and develop skills to fight?
- **Skills**. Will you study and pursue training to develop ministry skills and understanding?
- **Ministry**. When an opportunity to do ministry comes along, do you embrace the opportunity even if seems "beyond" you?

Early Days

If you stay in God's training program, you may feel like David's men in the Cave of Adullam – tired and unappreciated. You may even feel attacked, by both friends and enemies. But all this is intended by God as preparation for what is ahead, for victories, for fruitfulness, and resting in Kingdom life.

We recommend these books for more information on God's preparation for leadership:

The Making of a Leader, by J. Robert Clinton

Secrets of the Vine, by Bruce Wilkinson

Life Lessons

Most of the lessons orchestrated by Holy Spirit will not look like lessons. They will look like ordinary, everyday events. God sends opportunities for growth and development disguised as mundane occasions. Such opportunities might be an encounter in the grocery store, a conversation on the way out of a church meeting, or a trip with your family. It's only in looking back on these events that you realize God has orchestrated a spiritual lesson.

Team Ministry

In the 1990s, I was part of a small group of five men who committed to offer a teaching series. Our goal was to give a series of teachings on basic discipleship topics. We aimed to offer it in live seminars in local retreat settings. We also wanted to record live video to show on community TV stations. This was time-consuming work: preparing and practicing teachings, shooting video in the local community TV studio, editing the video to the exact lengths required, and more. We called this seminar series, *Christ in You, the Hope of Glory*, based on Colossians 1:27. In total, our team of five offered twenty-one hours of teaching in fifteen sessions.

This side of eternity we will not know the impact of this seminar. Dozens came to the live retreats, and perhaps hundreds watched the video teachings, which eventually played on a TV station in Minneapolis. After a few years, we wound down the project and moved on to new assignments in God. But as I reflected afterward on what God did with this seminar, it seemed to be another class in the school of the Spirit about how to work together as a team. Getting five leaders together and coming to agreement on the many details of this project was a major challenge. Some of us found it easy to be offended and had to learn God's way of dealing with that. We learned to handle differences in theology, differences in personality and working style, and more. These are valuable lessons for ministry and church leadership.

Early Days

The School of Christ

If someone asked you what book had most impacted you (besides the Bible), what would you say? Our pastor once asked the leadership team to list the books which had most impacted us. For me, one of the most meaningful books I've read is *The School of Christ*, by T. Austin-Sparks, a British pastor. This book was first published early in the last century. After going out of print, it was re-published by David Wilkerson in the 1990s.

I am convinced that God brings books (and other opportunities) into our lives when we need them and when we're ready for them. The message of *The School of Christ* is that God brings us to a *crisis*, a moment in time where he offers us a choice. The choice will often be a decision, for example, to accept or commit to God's offer of salvation (the terminology will vary according to one's theology). Life may include many such "crisis" moments, when we are walking the path of life and come to a "Y" or a crossroads, and must choose to go to the left or the right. Although Austin-Sparks used the term crisis, we would call it a decision point.

But the crisis is followed by a *process*. Both are essential to a life well-lived. The crisis is a moment in time, but the process occupies the rest of our life. Having said "yes" to Christ, we enter a school, where the subject is Christ, and the teacher is the Holy Spirit. Of course, Holy Spirit is teaching and training us in the ways of God.

Training in the ways of God has very little to do with learning doctrine, which is often the focus of discipleship for new believers. Rather, this school of the Holy Spirit is designed to teach us what we need to know to walk with God and to fulfill our calling in God. Thus, each of us will have a customized curriculum designed by the Holy Spirit to fit us.

Knowing God by Experience

A primary purpose of Holy Spirit in this school is to help us get to know God better. God wants us to know him by experience. Many of us can remember a dramatic encounter with God during an altar call. God also reveals himself through people, although we don't always recognize these times. If you wonder whether God is engaging with you during an experience, ask yourself if you feel loved in that moment. God delights in giving you a love encounter.

Scripture points to this reality.

> *And this is eternal life, that they know you the only true God, and Jesus Christ whom you have sent. John 17:3 (ESV)*

Theology tells us about God by describing his attributes – who he is. It can be helpful to know that God is omnipotent, (all-powerful), or omniscient (all-knowing). One of my friends sums up such attributes by saying, "God is big!"

Early Days

Theology also tells about God through his names. God reveals himself in more than a dozen ways, including *Jehovah Jireh*, our Provider, *Jehovah Rapha*, our Healer, and *Jehovah Tsidkenu*, our Righteousness.

These descriptions of who God is are all helpful. But for me, the most powerful way to experience God is through what he does.

In the next section, "Experiencing God," I describe five ways I encountered and still experience the living God.

- Father
- Gardener
- Master Planner
- Protector
- Healer

Of course, God is much more than this to me, and presents himself in other roles to other people. But these are five of the ways I have come to know God.

Experiencing God

Jesus said that eternal life is as simple as knowing God (John 17:3). We get to know him by experiencing him in the midst of life. This section identifies several ways I have come to know God by experience.

Father

The summer between sixth and seventh grades was one of my best summers ever. Like most boys, I had enjoyed building model airplanes – plastic and glue and decals and a bit of paint. These kits came in a box with a picture and assembly instructions, which I followed closely (that's the way I was). But then I discovered model airplanes that could fly – with a gas motor and wings and a control line to keep them from going wild. This was back before radio-controlled airplanes, or at least before I could afford one of those. So, I spent most of my hard-earned allowance on a piper cub – all plastic, except for the engine. With my Dad's help, we got some fuel in the tank, started the engine, and then let 'er go. Alas, after a couple of weeks of boyhood bliss, my plane crashed, breaking into a dozen pieces. Like Humpty Dumpty, my plane would not go back together.

After some research into my options, I learned that I could build a bigger airplane from light-weight wood. So, I bought the kit, assembled the plane, and pondered where I could go to fly. This plane had a wingspan of a yard, compared to the much smaller plastic plane that died a painful death. As a result, it needed a circle fifty feet in diameter, much more than my front yard offered (we had lots of trees). I found an empty field a block away, obtained permission to use it, and then mowed down a swath of grass big enough to fly my new plane. The grass was tall, a foot or two, and needed frequent mowing, but with nearby houses a hundred yards away, I had found the perfect spot.

Soon the day finally arrived to fire up the engine and fly my new plane. I stood in the center of the circle, with two nylon strings running from the handle in my hand to the plane, to control the elevator at the back of the plane. All I had to do was tilt the handle up to make the plane go up, or tilt it down to make the plane go down. I started up the engine while someone held the plane, then I ran out to the center of the circle, picked up the handle, and waited for my helper to let the plane go. After a couple of bounces in the short grass, my plane was up and away.

We often had visitors to my circle in the field, as many as a dozen kids. I became quite proficient, and over time let my friends fly my plane. The circle was big enough that none of us "pilots" ever got dizzy. With a little practice, we could make the plane go up and around in a tight loop and reverse course, flying upside down. My favorite stunt was to turn the plane straight up and over my head, and then as it dove towards the ground on the other side of the circle, pull it out of the dive and resume the flight.

But boys and risk often go together. One time I waited too long to pull my plane out of its nosedive, and

Father

we crashed. I tried to repair the broken parts, and wood was easier to repair than plastic. But my plane was never the same. Even so, I had spent an entire summer treasuring my life as a pilot.

Spiritual Lessons

As I reflect on this experience, I see God teaching many lessons. Of course, he was doing more than that. He was delighting in me as his son. John Eldredge wrote of this phase of life in his book, *Fathered by God*. This book is full of insights about six stages of growth men go through to become who God designed them to be. This phase of my life was one of the early stages, the Cowboy stage.

In my experience with gas model airplanes, I learned the joy of building. I learned the value of hard work in the pursuit of a goal. I learned how to deal with disappointment. And best of all, I experienced God as Father, who delighted in me.

Gardener

My wife and I have tried to cultivate gardens many times. We've grown corn and tomatoes and several other kinds of vegetables. But neither of us have a "green thumb," so the results are mixed. Even so, we have a great appreciation for farmers and gardeners and anyone who grows food to eat or drink.

In John 15, Jesus describes Father as the gardener, the farmer, the vinedresser. He identifies himself as a vine, and each of us as branches. Jesus then describes how Father nurtures each of us.

Many great messages have been spoken and written about this word picture. One of the best is *Secrets of the Vine*, by Bruce Wilkinson. In this book, Wilkinson describes how Father brings to our lives what we need. What we need depends on whether our lives show no fruit, some fruit, more fruit, or much fruit. In his wisdom, God may use discipline, pruning of activities and priorities, or training in values and personal identity. Ultimately Father wants to bring us into a place of intimacy, a place of all-day attentiveness to Holy Spirit.

Learning to know God in this role has been very encouraging to me. No one enjoys pruning when it happens. But when you see the fruit that results afterward, you can only rejoice in the goodness of God.

Master Planner

Most evangelical Christians know of the tract titled *Four Spiritual Laws*, by Bill Bright of Campus Crusade for Christ. As a teenager, I used this tract for witnessing on a university campus.

One key phrase from the tract is that God has a wonderful plan for your life. Of course, as described in that tract, the plan is for salvation. Yet the Bible is clear that God's plan for each life includes more than that.

> *For I know the plans I have for you," says the LORD. "They are plans for good and not for disaster, to give you a future and a hope. Jeremiah 29:11 (NLT)*

Sometimes we only see God's plan when looking back on events. Two of the key decisions in anyone's life are who to marry (if they marry), and what job to take. In my case, I have seen God sovereignly intervene in my life to make sure I got those decisions right. He did so in a way that did not violate my free will. That is the wonder of our sovereign God – he works out his will in our lives while preserving our free choice to make decisions.

My Wife

Very few of us meet our future spouse when arriving home from a day at work. But that's what happened to me. I was working a summer job at the time, between my junior and senior years at college. When I arrived home, four strangers were seated in our living room.

Experiencing God

Two of them were friends of my parents, from a city an hour away in northeast Ohio. One of them was a very cute young woman about my age, along with her mother. My parents and their friends were going to an outdoor concert of the Cleveland Symphony Orchestra. But the plan hit a snag when friends from Canada dropped in to stay with the friends of my parents. My mom told them to "bring them along."

We all enjoyed dinner in our home. Somehow my dad managed to ask the young woman from Canada and her mother if it would be okay if I drove her to the concert. And then he found a moment to ask me if I wanted to do that. I said yes – the first and only "arranged" date in my life. We drove off in my '65 Mustang and enjoyed the concert and a pizza afterward. I brought her back in plenty of time to return with her mom and their friends. At that point, I never thought I'd see her again.

But my dad continued the matchmaker role. A day or two later, he mentioned that the young lady was still staying with friends, and I could probably arrange a date to see her if I was interested. I was. So, I picked her up, and we spent a day on the beach at Presque Isle, Pennsylvania, and then at an amusement park north of Pittsburgh. I was smitten. So was she.

Events proceeded rapidly. Even though I returned to college in Iowa that fall, and she moved to a new home in northern Minnesota, we managed to see each other two times in the fall. We got engaged in January and married in April. A whirlwind romance, to be sure,

Master Planner

and one that has endured now for almost 50 years, growing stronger every year.

My dad, a pastor, presided over our wedding. Not long after we were married, he told my wife that the moment she set foot in our home, he knew she would be my future wife. I'm sure he enjoyed "helping God" work out the arrangements.

My Job

Every job we choose to take is important, but the first job is especially important. I chose the field of urban planning for a career. After graduation in 1973, I went to a job fair in Atlanta at the national conference for my profession. This job fair offered the best chance of finding a good job.

As I went around from table to table with my resume, I felt confident about my prospects. One of the available jobs was with the city of Mankato, in southern Minnesota. The interviewer asked if I would meet with him privately at the end of the day. My wife was with me, and we met with him before the dinner hour. He told me the job was mine if I wanted it. But the salary he offered was the lowest of any of the jobs for which I had interviewed. He knew the salary was a barrier, but it was the best he could do. He also knew I was likely to get other offers, and he asked me to give him my response within the hour, so he could offer the job to someone else if I didn't want it.

My wife and I stepped away to talk about it. We had been living on a bare-bones budget for some time, while

Experiencing God

I went to grad school. During that season, it was a special treat to go out once a month to McDonald's for dinner. At that point in our lives, it did not occur to us to pray about it. I turned down the offer.

In the end, I received six job offers from this job fair. I took the one up in Florida. The salary was almost twice that of the job I was offered in Minnesota. But nothing was right about the job, and I ended up leaving after a year and a half.

When I left, I went to the national conference job fair that year, which was in Vancouver, BC. I had only three interviews, and only one offer, in Minnesota, which I accepted. God was narrowing the options, to get me where he wanted me.

Several years later I took a different job in Minnesota which allowed me to listen to a Christian radio program while driving to work. One day while listening during my drive, God spoke to my spirit. He revealed that at the job fair in Atlanta, he wanted me to take the low-paying job, the one in Mankato, Minnesota, not the one in Florida.

This revelation was in the early 1980s. And then in the early 1990s, God moved me to Mankato, Minnesota, in an unrelated sequence of events.

Today I stand amazed. God wanted me in Mankato in 1973, and through a sovereignly arranged sequence of events, he moved me there in 1992.

When I look back on what God has done in my life, I can only rejoice in God and his ability to get me where he wants me to be.

Protector

For twenty years we lived next to the National Guard Armory in Mankato, Minnesota. This was an armored unit, and our kids loved to see their tanks drive up the ramp out of the armory basement.

One night we woke up to the sound of a car crashing into the building next door to us. We quickly donned outdoor clothes and walked over to see what was up. The police were there, with lights flashing. They had been chasing this car. As they pulled up, they saw the driver fleeing the scene.

In the daylight of the next morning, we discovered the rest of the story. The National Guard kept a couple of vans parked in front of the armory. One of them had been flipped 90 degrees after being hit by the car that crashed into our neighbor a few seconds later.

We also saw skid marks on the pavement and in the grass in front of our house that told the rest of the tale. Our front yard was only about 20 feet deep. This included 10 feet of grass and shrubs next to our house, the public sidewalk, and the boulevard next to the street, which sported a beautiful tree. We always parked our van near the front corner of our house, and our car at the curb.

After spotting these clues, we determined the sequence of the car that crashed. While being chased by the police, the driver had turned a corner too wide, smashed into a van in front of the armory, skidded a few feet behind our van, somehow stayed on the sidewalk while missing the tree and our car, and then smashed

Experiencing God

into the building next door to our house. It would have been very easy for this out-of-control car to smash into our van or house, smash into our car, take out the tree, or all of these. Instead, the car navigated a perfect path for us, leaving only marks on the grass.

We had always felt there was an angel or two protecting our family and our property. I have no other explanation for events that night. We experienced God as Protector in a big way

Rescuer

The year 1992 brought major changes to our family. We moved from the inner city of Minneapolis to Mankato, a small city in south-central Minnesota. We moved from a home we owned to a rented duplex apartment. We moved from a nice-paying job to self-employment. In retrospect, I see God's hand in this, simplifying our life. When you have almost no money, you really notice when God shows up with exactly what you need. On two separate occasions in this season, we were literally down to our last $2, with no bank accounts and no credit cards. Each time, God came through as our Provider.

In this season of "living by faith," we elected to drive east for a vacation with my brother in Ohio. The plan was to spend a week in his cabin at a church camp, at very low cost. We took most of our cash, about $400, enough to cover gas and fast food meals on the way. On our first day, we stopped for lunch at a McDonald's in Rochester, Minnesota. We enjoyed our meal, collected our four kids and diaper bag, and returned to our van. I pulled out of our parking space and stopped near the

Protector

restaurant to deposit a little trash from our car. At that very moment, a McDonald's worker came out to our van carrying my wife's purse, with the $400 cash we needed for the trip! In the busyness of returning to our van, we had left the purse in clear view next to the window. God rescued us!

Experiencing God

Healer

We have experienced God as Healer many times. God sometimes heals instantaneously, and sometimes gradually. When one of our daughters was about seven years old, she was playing baseball with two friends who played Little League. She was pitching, and the ball came off the bat straight into her eye. We prayed immediately and then headed to the emergency room. Our daughter went home with a patch over her eye, and we scheduled an appointment with an ophthalmologist, an MD who specializes in eye care.

The ophthalmologist indicated she was blind in that eye, and there was nothing he could do. Naturally, we asked family and church friends to pray. Her eye began to improve gradually, and a year later the ophthalmologist reported that she had 20-20 vision.

At that point, he also told my wife that he never expected her eye to improve. He reported that when he had first seen her, he had no hope. Our daughter continues to have perfect vision to this day.

Healing Ministry

This incident happened in the year 2000, shortly after we attended a prophetic conference in St. Paul, Minnesota. At the end of the first night, my wife, Deb, and I were getting ready to leave the conference to drive home. One of the leaders of the conference, Ian Andrews, approached us. Ian has a healing ministry that is well known in England. He said God had asked him to pray over us and impart to us the gifts of healing and word of knowledge. Naturally, we were delighted to receive his prayer.

One of our friends observed this prayer and bought us a vial of anointing oil. Several years went by before we began to see Ian's prayer make a difference in our lives. We discovered a teaching series by Bill Johnson, of Bethel Church in Redding, CA. Eventually, we began praying for people in home groups and at the altar in church meetings. (When I say praying, I include commanding and declaring, as Jesus taught the disciples. See Acts 3:6.) We sought out the healing rooms in Redding and in Spokane, WA, partly to receive prayer for our own needs, but also to learn from those who prayed for us.

After a few years, we began to offer healing prayer for people that we encountered on the streets. Some people are reluctant to receive prayer, but most are happy to have you pray for them.

God has continued to teach and nurture this gift in us. We were grateful for the prophetic prayer from Ian Andrews in the year 2000. We have pursued healing ministry, especially since moving to the state of Washington in 2012. Shortly after that move, God introduced us to a group that meets weekly for healing prayer, and we learned much from them. In 2015 we published a small booklet titled "Healing Is For Today." This booklet offers scriptures and quotes from healing ministers of the past 100 years (www.HealingIsForToday.net). We have taken a healing ministry team to local churches in central Washington.

Growth

Jesus is the author and finisher of our faith (Hebrews 12:2). That doesn't mean we are passive. This section pursues the role we play in growing to maturity.

Shepherding the Vision

My wife and I moved from Florida to Minnesota in our early 30s. Yes, that's the opposite direction most people would choose. But I had landed a good job, and we had good memories of Minnesota. We knew the winters would be cold, and decided to fight back by learning to enjoy winter. We did that. We took up cross-country skiing.

Our early efforts at skiing were casual. We took a lesson or two, found a local golf course with easy trails, and learned to kick-and-glide. It was fun. Before long, we found some neighbors who also liked to ski, and started looking for a bigger challenge. Eventually, we discovered a cross-country ski resort located four hours north of us. They named it Maplelag because of all the maple trees. To supplement the maple sugar business, they built a lodge and several small cabins and carved ski trails through the rolling terrain.

Our friends and we began to visit Maplelag often and became proficient at skiing. They held a short ski race every February, and in 1983 my wife, Deb, won her class.

Shepherding the Vision

Winters in the Midwest are long, and both Minnesota and Wisconsin have ski races patterned after the big ski races in Scandinavia. Minnesota has the Vasaloppet, and Wisconsin has the Birkebeiner. These ski races are at least 55 kilometers (33 miles) in length, although both offer a shorter distance option.

Skiing 33 miles is a marathon experience, although not as difficult as running the original 26.2-mile marathon. To finish in a reasonable time, it was necessary for me to ski more, both to improve skills, and to develop strength and endurance. With the arrival of our third child, it was time to "retire" from ski marathons. By that time, I had skied the Birkebeiner five times.

Spiritual Lessons

For me, skiing had started as a strategy to "attack" winter, with a bonus of fun times with friends. When I put my skis in storage, I realized that God was using this experience to teach me spiritual lessons.

- Distract yourself from the negative in life by pursuing positive experiences.
- Set a goal that is ambitious but still feasible.
- Set up milestones that take you small steps in the right direction.
- Mix the less pleasant times (hard exercise) with fun times (breakfast with friends beforehand).

My experience with marathons provided inspiration in the mid-1990s, when I was part of a group of friends who decided to put on a teaching seminar. We called it *Christ in You, the Hope of Glory*. By the time we were

Growth

done, we had delivered a three-part, 21-hour teaching series at several facilities in southern Minnesota. We also ran the series on two TV stations, including one in Minneapolis.

For a time, I forgot about my experience with marathons. But in 2010 a brother in the Lord and I, plus our wives, were visiting a ministry couple in Wyoming. Before our departure, the pastor in Wyoming spoke prophetically to us with a verse that points directly to a marathon.

> *Write the vision And make it plain on tablets, That he may run who reads it. For the vision is yet for an appointed time; But at the end it will speak, and it will not lie. Though it tarries, wait for it; Because it will surely come, It will not tarry. Habakkuk 2:2-3 (NKJV)*

This word was and is a tremendous encouragement to me. Since 2010, I have continued writing in my journals. But writing for others has been rare. This book, *Rivers in the Desert*, finally assembles my thoughts on themes that have been important for the past thirty years.

It's easy to give up when you see little reinforcement of the ideas God has been giving you. There is no way to know what the future will bring. But I remember once, in the middle of a time of discouragement, a leader from England saying to me, "Don't stop running until you hit the tape." This is great advice, which I am doing my best to follow.

You Are the Portrait of the Assignment

For most of us the word "assignment" brings back memories of school, homework, deadlines, and employment. But what if God gives us assignments designed to help us pursue the dream and destiny he has designed for us? I believe that's exactly what he does. I explored this pattern in the chapter, "The School of Christ."

We all had easier assignments in third grade than in tenth grade. In the same way, God gives us easier assignments at the beginning of our walk with him. The early assignments are few and simple. He wants us to make a space in our day for a quiet time, time with God. He wants us to find a good church, one that preaches the Bible and offers opportunities for fellowship with fellow believers. These are lessons we never leave behind. They serve as a foundation for later growth in Christ, in the same way that learning addition and multiplication serves as a foundation for algebra.

At some point, God will begin to give you assignments different from your fellow believers. All believers are to serve and love others. But some need to learn specific roles, such as shepherding or teaching. If God is calling you as a shepherd to his church, he will give you many opportunities to care for and watch over others. If God is calling you as a teacher to his church, he will give you desire to read and skills for study, and little by little, put you in teaching situations.

These two roles, shepherd and teacher, are named in Ephesians 4:11. Most of us recognize those who operate

Growth

in these gifts. But it is more accurate to say that these people *are* gifts. In other words, a teacher may be gifted in teaching, but he or she became that way by carrying out assignments from God.

To put it another way, God gave this person a series of assignments that made them what they are today. Along the way, this person said "yes" to God many times, given the challenges and opportunities that appeared at various points along the way. In a very real way, God has made them what they are. In other words, God has made them into what he called them to be, their destiny.

I am using the role of teacher as an example. It's easy to see that God might prepare one person to teach in Sunday School, another to teach in a Bible college, and other to write. None of these variations in teaching are better or worse, higher or lower. We simply become what God has intended us to be, a unique calling in the church.

In this sense, an assignment is a stepping-stone to your calling in Christ. Each assignment is hand-crafted by God to shape and grow you. You are the portrait of the assignment.

Finish Well

The goal of our faith is maturity. We all want to finish well, to hear "well done, good and faithful servant" from our Lord. This section points to that goal.

The Race

> *Therefore, since we are surrounded by such a huge crowd of witnesses to the life of faith, let us strip off every weight that slows us down, especially the sin that so easily trips us up. And let us run with endurance the race God has set before us. Hebrews 12:1 (NLT)*

In the past decade, I read three books authored by established leaders about finishing the race. All offered the warning that not all leaders finish well. One teacher pointed to the lesson of the kings of Israel in the Old Testament. The writer of Chronicles often ends the account of a given king with a summary – he followed God, or he didn't. Too many did not finish well.

In the 1980s two authors published books titled, *The Making of a Leader*. One of these was J. Robert (Bobby) Clinton, a professor at Fuller Theological Seminary. In his research, Clinton examined the lives of forty-nine church leaders of the past century. He concluded that only thirteen finished well. That means that only one out of three or four finished well.

Finish Well

Clinton went further, offering insight from the lives of leaders who did finish well. He lists several factors that enhance the prospect of finishing well.

- A lifetime perspective on ministry
- Times of intimacy with God for renewal
- Personal disciplines that support intimacy and perseverance
- A posture of lifelong learning
- Maintain relationship with mentors

For anyone wanting to shepherd a vision, this is good advice, at any time of their life.

What's in a Name?

Everyone loves to hear their name spoken. Dale Carnegie, the sales guru, wrote that one secret of success is to use the name of the person you're talking with. It works – whether you're trying to sell a product, or talking about the Kingdom.

Do people pronounce your name correctly? If you have one of the most popular last names in America, Smith or Johnson, everyone will get your name right. But I grew up with the last name, Rosebaugh, that I rarely heard pronounced the right way (the "gh" is silent, so it is rose-baw). For some reason, most people insert an *n* in the middle, or an *m* on the end, which changes the sound and the meaning.

Hebrew names have specific meanings. In Old Testament Hebrew culture, your name defined you – your nature, your character. Consider Abraham. His original name was Abram, which means exalted father. But when God made a covenant promise to him, he changed his name. God inserted into Abram's name an extra sound, *ah*, part of God's name, Yahweh. The result, Abraham, means father of nations. In a sense, God changed his destiny and then changed his name to reflect his destiny.

God did this again with Jacob. Jacob's original name meant grasper or usurper. This pointed to Jacob's destiny. At birth, he grasped the heel of his older brother, Esau. As the brothers became adults, Jacob tricked Esau out of his birthright, and then his blessing, thus usurping the place of his older brother. In time God dealt with

Finish Well

Jacob's character, to the point of crippling him in a wrestling match. At that point, God gave him the name Israel, which means prince of God. The nation that grew out of the loins of this man was called Israel.

Have you ever researched your ancestors, either on the Internet or by going to places they lived and looking at birth and marriage records? Many of us have. For most of my life, all I knew of my ancestors was a written account of an interview with my paternal grandfather. In his final years in a nursing home, a volunteer sat down with him and asked him about his ancestors. I am blessed by what she did, and thankful that my grandfather could remember so much of his past.

My Name

But one detail of my past remained unknown for decades – the meaning of my last name. I knew it was German, with "baugh" being the Anglicized version of "bach." A breakthrough came in a conversation with a German missionary, who asked me about my name. He told me "bach" is German for a stream or small river. Of course, "rose" points to the well-known flower.

With this understanding of the meaning of my name, I looked back at a prophetic word given to us on two occasions. The first time was in 1990 by a friend in Minnesota. The second time was in 2007 by a prophetic leader, Kris Vallotton, while we were visiting Bethel Church in Redding, California. As spoken by Kris, the word is that we would be streams-rivers in the desert, an oasis, an artesian spring.

What's in a Name?

The original word, from our friend in Minnesota, came from Isaiah 43:18-20. He said we would be walking a narrow path alongside a river in the desert, a river of refreshing. We are called to share those waters with others in the wilderness, and show them the path.

This word impacted us so strongly that I asked an artistic friend to sketch a picture of an oasis in the desert, which she was happy to do. This sketch hangs framed on the wall of our dining room. I asked for these verses to be penned under the sketch.

> *Behold, I will do a new thing; now it shall spring forth; shall ye not know it? I will even make a way in the wilderness. And it shall be called The way of holiness; Isaiah 43:19, Isaiah 35:8 (NKJV)*

> *I give waters in the wilderness, and rivers in the desert, to give drink to my people, my chosen. The wilderness and the solitary place shall be glad for them; and the desert shall rejoice, and blossom as the rose. Isaiah 43:20, Isaiah 35:1 (NKJV)*

With the help of our German friend, we now see the significance of our name. It points directly to the prophetic call and destiny on our lives, a call shared by many others, of course. Hence the name of this book – *Rivers in The Desert*. It also points to the purpose of this book – to offer living water to those in dry places.

Revival in Minnesota
by David Smith

This section highlights the personal story of David Smith. His close walk with God began in a 1971 revival in Minneapolis. In the 1980s, David served as an elder in the Jesus People Church. He now lives in Mankato.

Minneapolis Miracle

In October 1971, I was seventeen years old and on my way to a weekend prayer retreat at Camp Courage just west of Minneapolis. That weekend Dick Eastman used the gift of word of knowledge to call out almost a hundred youth one-by-one. He told them what God had called them to do, recalling events and conversations earlier in their life.

I received the baptism of the Holy Spirit on Friday night, along with at least 30 others. The rest of that weekend was supernatural. They closed the dining hall because none of the 120 students were showing up for meals. Curfew was dropped because young men and women were staying up all night in prayer, searching their hearts and seeking God.

We sought the Lord continuously for three days, from Friday evening until Sunday at noon. God was present in a tangible way as the Spirit hovered over our camp. We all left there changed by the power of the Holy Spirit.

Minneapolis Miracle

The speaker that weekend was Dick Eastman. On Monday, he went to North Central Bible College in downtown Minneapolis, to lead their morning chapel service. That chapel service lasted for three days, from Monday 8 AM to Wednesday 7 PM. The Bible school was shaken to its core. Scores of students were baptized in the Holy Spirit. Nightly meetings were held at the Minneapolis Gospel Tabernacle (Assemblies of God) on 13th Avenue, a few doors south of Lake Street in South Minneapolis. Here is a photo of the North Central Bible Institute, as it was known in the mid-20th century.

Dick left Minneapolis that Thursday. He had only been in town for seven days. He later wrote the details of that week in a book titled, *The Purple Pig and Other Miracles*.

That same night Brian Ruud, a young Canadian evangelist with a curly blond Afro, came to Minneapolis. He began nightly evangelistic meetings at Souls Harbor, located in the historic Lyceum Theater on 11th Street in downtown Minneapolis. Orchestra Hall is now

**Revival in Minnesota
by David Smith**

located on that site. Here is an aerial view of the Lyceum Theatre and a 1972 photo of Brian Ruud.

Those meetings continued seven days a week for seventeen weeks. Hundreds, perhaps thousands, were saved over that four-month period. The meetings ended when the holidays came and went, but not before shaking the Bible schools and impacting the church throughout the city. The revival meetings ended almost as suddenly as they started. But the move of God was still at work underground. Churches that are still with us today were planted coming out of that move of God in 1971.

Jesus People Church

One of the churches that came out of Souls Harbor in this move of God was Jesus People Church, which had a strong evangelistic anointing. When it later imploded in 1985-6, the transition launched at least 30 churches of around 300 each. One group remained and built a new building in a corn field in Eagan, MN.

1992 (Twenty-One Years Later)

I came to the Mankato region at the Lord's direction. I visited a home church in Good Thunder, and at that service, I saw a vision but could not interpret it immediately. Once I did gain understanding, I was asked back to share with the church what the Lord had revealed.

While I was sharing that vision, God told me, "Tell them I am bringing revival to this city." So, I told them what he said. Then God said, "They don't understand the scope of what you are saying. Tell them they do not understand the scope of what you are saying." I told them, and as I did the Lord whispered to me, "And neither do you." At that instant, I saw a bright flash of light. I cannot articulate what I saw in that flash of light, but whatever it was it left me speechless for several seconds to half a minute. That message and the impact of what my spirit saw grew into an invitation to come and watch him take this city and make it into a city of refuge. So, I moved here the following year, almost one year to the very day.

1999 (Twenty-Eight Years Later)

A visiting speaker from Missouri asked my pastor to invite me to join them after the meeting. He began the conversation by telling me about a revival that had happened in Minneapolis back in 1971. He had no idea I had been there for those meetings. He went on to say that

that revival had been miscarried, but that God was going to bring it back and bring it to full term. I thanked him for the encouragement and let him know I was physically there in 1971, and that God had told me he was going to complete what he had started.

2001 (Thirty Years Later)

A friend let me know that Brian Ruud was coming back to Minnesota in October. He was scheduled to speak in the Twin Cities. I told my friend, "If God is going to finish the Minneapolis Miracle revival in Mankato, then Brian Ruud will change his schedule and come to Mankato as well." And I prayed along those lines. A week later my friend told me Brian was indeed coming to Mankato, for one night only. I went to the meeting and afterward I was able to tell him how much his meetings in 1971 had impacted me at the age of 17 as well as the region. In further conversation, we determined that he came to Mankato on the 30th anniversary of his first night of ministry back in 1971 in Minneapolis.

2013 (Forty-Two Years Later)

Another friend sent me a copy of the book, *The Purple Pig and Other Miracles*. For the first time, I read about the encounter from the vantage point of the speaker, Dick Eastman.

August 2015 (Forty-Four Years Later)

I met a young man one morning, at the Potter's House of Prayer in Mankato, who said to me, "Do you know what my favorite book is, other than the Bible?" When I told him "No," he said, "The Purple Pig." After he raved for a while about the book, I asked him, "Have you read about the Minneapolis Miracle?" When he said "Yes," I told him, "I was there." He said, "Shut up. No way!"

August 2016 (Forty-Five Years Later)

At the PHOP Prayer Summit, I got a "Minnesota Miracle" hoodie. These were made specifically for that conference because of a word at the prophetic conference in October 2015. God said, "I am making the Minnesota River Valley a valley of miracles." The hoodie recalls that word and the event that happened 45 years earlier in Minneapolis. His sign to me in 2001 was that Brian Rudd altered his plans to visit Mankato on the 30th anniversary of the Minneapolis Miracle in 1971. But he came to Mankato to indicate that it has since become the Minnesota Miracle.

December 2017 (Forty-Six Years Later)

The final chapter of this story is still being written. God has promised to take this city. What God has started he will surely complete.

Jamie VanGelder, Senior Pastor at the House Church in Eagan, MN, received a vison of ten churches in ten cities along the Minnesota River Valley. He has prayer walked the entire length of the route my wife and I took when moving in 1993, starting in Dakota County and ending in Mankato. We believe we walked a prophetic path for revival 22 years before Jamie and his team

Revival in Minnesota
by David Smith

walked the same path. We see this as a confirmation. Jamie and the House Church worship in the building we built in 1987 as the Jesus People Church. This is the Jesus People Church that came out of the meetings at Souls Harbor in 1971.

Part Three
Rivers in Your Life

What Is Your Dream?

This section invites you to experience personally the rivers of life described in this book. I invite you to dream.

Two Kinds of Dreams

Several years ago, I sat among a dozen friends around a campfire enjoying a cool mountain evening. Our hostess asked us to share our dreams. Over the years I have recorded many nighttime dreams, and I shared a dream with images of a bus, a flood, the Statue of Liberty, and an island. Then I realized she wasn't asking about dreams in the night, but rather about our hopes and desires. Oops.

Everyone has a "pizza" dream now and then. In the same way, everyone has desires that pop up that are not from God. But over time, as we walk with God, our desires change. As this happens, God promises a reward.

> *Delight yourself in the LORD, and he will give you the desires of your heart. Psalm 37:4 (ESV)*

This is a dynamic process. God paints a picture of what is possible, and we say, "yes, I want that." Desire is born, and over time, blossoms and grows. God blesses us in many ways regardless of our desires – with provision, protection, the beauty of nature, and much more. But as our desires align more and more with

God's design for us, we find many of our desires being fulfilled. That is a profound blessing.

A Life Dream

Do you have a life dream? Young people often aim for a successful career, with marriage and a family. Older people often aim at a comfortable retirement, with time to relax and travel and be with children and grandchildren. These are all admirable goals, but there is more to life when we walk with God. Each of us is born a unique human being, like no other on earth. God has in mind projects and purposes designed uniquely for us.

> *For we are God's masterpiece. He has created us anew in Christ Jesus, so we can do the good things he planned for us long ago. Ephesians 2:10 (NLT)*

It's not always easy to know God's plans and purposes for us. Our desires can be a swirl of ideas. Some of these might be self-serving. Others can be "good" ideas that bring mixed results. Still others are God ideas that produce good results.

Sometimes our religious training gets in the way. We may think that an idea that serves others at our expense is a God idea. That is often true, but it is not necessarily true. We can spend seven days a week in church activities, only to find ourselves burned out, having neglected to spend time alone with God.

Religion can also teach us that an idea that blesses us, or which we enjoy, is of the "flesh." God is a good

What Is Your Dream?

father, and he wants us to enjoy friendship and fellowship, both with him and with each other.

God Nurtures Your Dream

Imagine yourself as a father with children who are emerging into their teenage years. You observe certain unique abilities and tendencies in each child. Suppose you have a son that likes to play ball and a daughter that likes gymnastics. You will be sure they have the right equipment, and you will do what you can to practice with them and help them find opportunities to grow in their skill.

Our heavenly Father is the same way. He puts certain interests and abilities in each one of us at birth. As we mature, he gives us opportunities to practice and perfect those gifts. Along the way, he will also put in our heart certain desires which align with our gifts. Those desires often take the shape of a dream, as we imagine what the future could bring.

For example, we might grow up reading books and studying topics that interest us. Over time we may gather a library of books, and develop skills in research and study. These tendencies may well line up with a calling in God to be a teacher. As we grow in that gifting, we will find pleasure in reading, writing, and speaking about the topics God has taught us.

This example fits my life. Every calling has its own pattern, where God first does in the natural what he eventually does in the spiritual (1 Corinthians 15:46). Think about what you've enjoyed doing over the years.

Your Life Dream

What is your life dream? Perhaps the best expression of this question comes from a book by John Eldredge, *Wild at Heart*. Eldredge stated it this way: If you had permission to do what you really want to do, what would you do? What is written on your heart? What makes you come alive? If you could do what you've always wanted to do, what would it be?

You have permission from God to dream!

Most of us encounter obstacles in pursuing our dream. Sometimes when a dream is delayed or frustrated, we wonder if the dream is from God or not.

> *Hope deferred makes the heart sick, but a dream fulfilled is a tree of life. Proverbs 13:12 (NLT)*

When a dream seems to be delayed, it is likely that the dream is simply taking time to be fulfilled, that God is at work bringing it to pass. If we feel a dream is from God, we should never give up.

In time, we learn to trust our heart, the heart that has been transformed by God. You can come to the place where you live by desire, asking yourself, "what do I want to do next?" Trust the result – it will take you forward in the path toward reaching your dream.

An Illustration

Perhaps a personal illustration will give you an idea of how a dream can grow. Our dream has been shaped by prophetic words brought to us over the last 25 years. As

What Is Your Dream?

described in "What's in a Name?" we received a prophetic word in 1992 about a ministry of "rivers in the desert." This word was a confirmed 15 years later by a recognized prophet.

Between these two "bookends," God brought increasing clarity to our destiny and life dream. Although you might think God would move us toward a full-time, paid ministry position, that's not what he did. Instead, God took us through a series of lessons on many topics, described in the chapter, "The School of Christ."

During this time, God took a fledgling business we had started in 1985 and brought a measure of prosperity. During this time, God made us aware of a movement toward "marketplace ministry." I shared details about this in the chapter, "Sharing Our Faith."

These ideas became a natural "home" for us as we pursued his call on our lives. At a retreat many years ago, I felt God say that our ministry is to equip those who come to the church building. Equip them for what? To function in the marketplace like the believers in Acts.

When God has a life message for you, he first makes you an example of that message. I explore that theme in the chapter, "You Are the Portrait of the Assignment." Holy Spirit teaches you by experience the lessons you need to know, and those are the lessons that you are intended to teach to others. You can only teach people a message when you live that message.

This is the path God has taken us, to give an understanding about our call and destiny. I offer this only as an illustration of what it's like to pursue a God-given dream. Everyone's path will be different.

What Is Your Ministry?

This section invites you to interpret your dream in terms of ministry. To help you break out of the box of tradition, we start with a new understanding of ministry.

Ministry Options

Even though all believers are called to be ministers, some choose a path that involves a ministry position. Often, such a position includes a salary, or at least some form of support, as in the case of foreign missionaries and others.

In many cases, someone pursuing a ministry position will become a pastor of a local church. Such a person typically does the teaching and preaching, coordinates other ministries, and handles a variety of administrative responsibilities.

The Bible doesn't seem to distinguish between those who hold ministry positions and those who don't. Paul worked as a tentmaker, although he clearly devoted most of his waking hours to ministry.

What are the options for a Christian to do ministry when they do not feel called to a ministry position? Most churches offer a variety of volunteer roles, such as teaching Sunday School, doing maintenance or clerical work, serving as an usher, being part of the worship team, or any of dozens of other roles. These are all important ministry functions within the local church, but there is more.

What Is Your Ministry?
Marketplace Ministers

The church needs marketplace ministers.

As measured by attendance, the church in America is in decline. Numbers are not the most important measure of the influence of the Kingdom. But in the same way that the significance of a river is measured not just by width but also by depth, the significance of a local church can be measured both by the width of attendance and by the depth of God's presence and power.

The goal of advancing the Kingdom outside the walls of the church is not new. The history of the early church is filled with ministry encounters in the marketplace.

A minister with a position in the church can preach and teach about marketplace ministry, but in that position, is not a portrait of the assignment. On the other hand, a person who is a marketplace minister does not have ready access to teach Christians in the church about marketplace ministry.

This seems a little bit like "Catch 22," a novel and movie fifty years ago about a man who wanted to leave the army. In that story, the army would let you out if you were crazy, but of course, if you wanted to get out you weren't crazy.

In this ministry dilemma, you can be a pastor with access every Sunday morning to a room full of Christians who are potential marketplace ministers. Or you can be a marketplace minister, but have little access to train other Christians. There are exceptions. A person with experience in marketplace ministry can decide to obtain ministry credentials, such as licensing or ordination. Or, in some churches, a person with experience in marketplace ministry might be able to preach or teach on occasion.

You Have Permission

God has given you permission to do ministry!

If you feel a call to fill a volunteer position in a local church, then obviously you will need both permission and approval from the authorities in that church. That's easy if there has been a request for volunteers. But if you would like to offer ministry that is not being requested, be careful. You should approach the church leaders to see if they welcome your efforts. If they do, continue to honor their place, and God will bless your efforts. If they don't, ask the Lord for clear direction about where he wants you to minster.

God has given you permission to do ministry. You may feel challenged to believe you can do ministry. But God has called each one of us to be ministers. We have looked at some of the barriers in this book: identity (you are like Christ), grace (you have power), equipping (practice doing ministry), and more. But you can overcome every barrier.

An Illustration

We first encountered the idea of marketplace ministry in the late 1990s, as described in the chapter, "Marketplace Ministry." We were further encouraged by the Seven Mountains message, outlined in the chapter "Seven Mountains."

What Is Your Ministry?

At first, we brought Christian principles to our business. We initiated prayer meetings in the workplace, for those who were interested. We crafted a statement of company vision and values that declared God first in the business and shared this with the entire staff.

Many churches undertake outreach activities. As our pastor encouraged us to "take it to the streets," we committed to outreach in our community with a group of like-minded Christians. Over time, we felt increasingly free as individuals to share our faith "on the streets," including praying for healing for people we encountered.

I explored how God makes you the message he wants you to give in the chapter, "You Are the Portrait of the Assignment." This is what God did in us for twenty-five years, opening our eyes to a new way of living our faith, 24/7/365, everywhere we went. We were stretched, but over time God changed us. We now have many stories to share of God's goodness and grace in the marketplace.

Pursuing Your Destiny

This section invites you to embrace the message of rivers in the desert. You have an important place – to drink of the river, and to invite others to the river.

Living Your Life Dream and Ministry

The message of this book is simple. God wants you in the ministry.

God is a loving Father. He has given you the nature of Jesus. He fills you with the power of Holy Spirit. He has done and will continue to do his part in the great "dance" of life.

Your part is to respond. You can choose from many opportunities. Most of them will be "part-time," here-and-there in the walk of life. As you've heard, "bloom where you are planted."

Stay tuned to God's voice to your heart. Try things. At first, not everything turns out as expected. Keep trying. God will give you hints and open doors as you go.

Find a small group where you can experience fellowship. Pursue opportunities to be equipped for ministry. Practice ministry. Be open to ministry where you work, shop, and play.

Guard your heart. If you encounter delays, continue to be persistent. Don't sit back and wait for a lightning bolt from heaven. God wants you to take the initiative. It may be difficult to find a balance between pushing and waiting. Pray about it. God is raising "adult" sons and daughters who can take the initiative.

Church and Ministry

We believe church occurs where you gather with other Christians. This can be a setting of two or twenty. It can be two hundred or two thousand. You may find ministry opportunities where you gather with other believers.

But there are many other ministry opportunities in places where you do not gather with other Christians. We can call this "outreach." Or we can call it "going," as we have done in this book. Either way, this is ministry.

Final Thoughts

If you find yourself in a dry place, the message of this book is for you. If you have a heart to reach out to others who live in dry places, this message is for you. Some of those living in dry places are believers who have given up hope in the church. Some are not yet believers. In both cases, you have living water to offer.

Ezekiel offers a beautiful picture of God's desire for you (Ezekiel 47:1-12). He describes water flowing from the temple, the presence of the Lord. The river grows deeper and deeper, and brings life to the desert where it flows. Everywhere it flows, it brings life and healing.

Bring life and healing to those around you. Jump in the river.

Proof

84600603R00085

Made in the USA
Columbia, SC
18 December 2017